THE BONFIRE OF THE VANITIES

Tom Wolfe

AUTHORED by Elizabeth Smith
UPDATED AND REVISED by W.C. Miller

COVER DESIGN by Table XI Partners LLC
COVER PHOTO by Olivia Verma and © 2005 GradeSaver, LLC

BOOK DESIGN by Table XI Partners LLC

Published by GradeSaver LLC, www.gradesaver.com

First published in the United States of America by GradeSaver LLC. 2007

ISBN 978-1-60259-089-2

Printed in the United States of America

Table of Contents

Table of Contents

Table of Contents

Biography of Tom Wolfe (1931–)

Thomas Kennerly Wolfe, Jr., was born in Richmond, Virginia, on March 2, 1931, the son of Thomas Kennerly and Helen (Hughes) Wolfe. He graduated from Washington and Lee University in 1951 and earned a doctorate in American studies at Yale University in 1957. Wolfe married Sheila Berger (art director of Harper's magazine) in 1978. They have two children: Alexandra and Thomas.

One of Wolfe's most important contributions to American letters is his journalism. He started in the business at the *Springfield Union* in Massachusetts before moving on to positions at *The Washington Post* and *The New York Herald Tribune*, where he was a feature writer. In 1963 Wolfe won wide recognition for a series of articles in *Esquire* and *New York*, the Sunday magazine of *The Herald Tribune.*

His work at these and other publications established Wolfe as one of the leading purveyors of The New Journalism –– a style of journalistic writing (which Wolfe himself dubbed) that used traditionally literary techniques, such as subjective points–of–view and lengthy dialogs, to energize non–fiction reportage. Some of Wolfe's articles in this vein were collected in his first book, *The Kandy–Kolored Tangerine–Flake Streamline Baby.*

Wolfe's intense observations of American life created a new kind of social commentary and revitalized the field of journalism. His style emphasized the increasing awareness of American diversity that developed in the sixties and seventies. Wolfe, with his highly erudite and often old–fashioned language, created interesting portraits of the youth drug culture, social justice movements, and changing social mores.

In 1968 Wolfe published *The Electric Kool–Aid Acid Test*, which followed novelist Ken Kesey and his drug–taking followers, the Merry Pranksters, on a cross–country bus trip. Wolfe later published *The Right Stuff* (1979), about the Apollo 7 astronauts, which told the story of NASA's concern with the psychological makeup of its astronauts. This book earned Wolfe both the American Book Award and the National Book Critics Circle Award in 1980.

Wolfe's *Bonfire of the Vanities* (1987) was a best–seller. Like most of his work, it was welcomed with mixed reviews. Critics tended to appreciate the energy of Wolfe's trenchant social commentary while pointing out the cartoonish, rather unconvincing nature of his characters. *Bonfire of the Vanities* was made into a movie in 1990, starring Tom Hanks, Melanie Griffith, and Bruce Willis. Wolfe's recent novels include *A Man in Full*, and *I Am Charlotte Simmons.*

About The Bonfire of the Vanities

The Bonfire of the Vanities, published in 1987, was the eleventh book and first novel by the famous journalist, author, and American Studies scholar Tom Wolfe. Previously, Wolfe had written non–fiction journalism and essays on American life such as *The Electric Kool–Aid Acid Test* and *The Right Stuff*; while fictional, *Bonfire of the Vanities* retains much of the social commentary evident in his earlier works. The work was originally published in serial form in *Rolling Stone* before it was released as a hardcover. It sold in droves, landing atop the New York Times Bestseller List for two months. *The Bonfire of the Vanities* is considered by some commentators to be the "definitive book of 1980s New York," characterized by biting satire and cutting criticism of the rapacious society of the Reagan years. It was made into a 1990 film directed by Brian de Palma.

The title refers to a ritual practiced during the Renaissance: the public burning of "vanity" objects such as secular books, mirrors, and extravagant clothing by conservative Catholics. The most famous burning of vanities happened in Italy, led by the cleric Savonarola. In the novel, the "bonfire" to which Wolfe alludes is the metaphorical burning of the vain pursuits of the protagonist's life as a result of criminal prosecution, and his crucifixion in the media as a "Park Avenue playboy." It is also a reference to the hypocrisy of the media and race relations in 1980s New York. Many of the characters in the novel were based partly or wholly on real people, such as Judge Kovitsky, Thomas Killian, and the Reverend Bacon. The climate of ethnic, racial, and class strife is exaggerated somewhat for the purposes of the story, but the world Wolfe created in *Bonfire of the Vanities* reflects many of the ugly social truths of the 1980s -- and of today.

Character List

Sherman McCoy

Wall Street golden boy, scion of old W.A.S.P. money, and self–described "Master of the Universe," Sherman has it all. His education, his mistress Maria Ruskin, his social circle: all are elite. He is also clearly prejudiced along ethnic, religious, social, economic, gender and racial lines.

Judy McCoy

Sherman's wife –– two years his senior. She has become the "social x–ray" style of Park Avenue wife. As soon as she knows of the possibility of Sherman's affair, she withdraws all affection.

Campbell McCoy

Sherman and Judy's six–year–old daughter.

John Campbell McCoy

Sherman McCoy's aging father. The former "lion" general partner of the law firm Dunning, Sponget, and Leach.

Celeste McCoy

Sherman's aristocratic mother.

Thomas Killian

Extremely slick, well–dressed, and fast–talking criminal defense lawyer for Sherman McCoy. He formerly worked in the District Attorney's office, but went into private practice to make money. His clients include the worst kind of rich criminals, including racketeers and drug dealers. A native Irish New Yorker, he attempts to redeem favors owed him by people in the criminal justice system to shield his clients.

Maria Ruskin

Sherman McCoy's mistress. She is a working–class girl from South Carolina who has used her attrativeness to marry well. Her husband is the extremely wealthy and aged Arthur Ruskin.

Abe Weiss

Jewish District Attorney for the borough of the Bronx. He is constantly angling for re–election, which nears as the novel begins. He is an excellent manipulator of the press, and cares far more about voter opinion than he does about justice. He has the gall, however, to pretend otherwise and to assume a idealistic tone with some of his employees. Larry Kramer is one of his assistant district attorneys, and Weiss directs him in the McCoy case.

Henry Lamb

The hit–and–run victim in the Sherman McCoy case. A high school student living in a housing project in the Bronx, he has managed to keep himself out of trouble and to stay in school. By the standards of his neighborhood, this makes him an honor student. Annie Lamb is his mother.

Mrs. Annie Lamb

The mother of Henry Lamb. She used to work for Reverend Bacon.

Peter Fallow

An alcoholic, plagiarizing, sponging layabout reporter from *The City Light* who breaks the Lamb case when Al Vogel feeds him information. He is British, and despises all things American. His first name, Peter, may be a broad hint to his crying "wolf" about the "Lamb" case. His coverage of the McCoy case wins him a Pulitzer Prize.

Lawrence Kramer

The Assistant DA assigned to the McCoy case. He is a fawning sycophant to DA Abe Weiss. His ultimate goals appear to be the advancement of his legal career and sexual conquests with women, not necessarily in that order. He is uneasy about his Jewish heritage and resists the responsibilities of family life.

Rhoda Kramer

The wife of ADA Lawrence Kramer. She has recently given birth to their first child, Joshua.

Joshua Kramer

Infant son of Lawrence and Rhoda.

Detective Martin

The Irish cop half of the detective team of Martin and Goldberg. Kramer considers him the epitome of "Irish Masculinity."

Detective Goldberg

The Jewish detective assigned to the McCoy case. Kramer, who is Jewish himself, thinks he has become Irish by association with Martin.

Bernie Fitzgibbon

The Irish head of the homocide unit of the office of the District Attorney.

Freddie Button

Sherman McCoy's family lawyer. He works for Sherman's father's firm, Dunning, Sponget, and Leach. His name may be an reference to Red Buttons, the American comedian.

Sir Gerald Steiner

Jewish–British publisher of *The City Light.* Called "The Dead Mouse" by Fallow and his cronies. An early parody of the Rupert Murdoch–style of British journalism tycoon. The name Steiner is derived from a German word meaning "stone," which may refer either to Sir Gerald's implacability, or to Fallow's assumption that Steiner is not very bright.

Gene Lopwitz

Jewish head of the investment firm Pierce and Pierce. His name (lop–wits) is a crude reference to Wolfe's opinion of this type of Wall Street tycoon.

Al Vogel

A New York lawyer representing Henry Lamb in the McCoy case. He breaks the news to Peter Fallow, thus making the case public.

Filippo Chirazzi

A painter in the fashionable art world of New York. He is the paramour of Maria Ruskin and becomes her second husband.

Edward Fiske III

A young man, of Ivy League education, employed by the Episcopalian Diocese of New York to check on its donations to Reverend Bacon.

Reverend Bacon

A Harlem minister who wields great power within his African–American community. He is the head of several shell or dummy organizations and corporations, through which he practices extortion and fraudulently obtains monetary donations. He, like Abe Weiss, is a master manipulator of the press. He takes up the McCoy case as a means to attack the white power structure of Manhattan. Bacon's name is a direct attack on the "pork–barrel" money he extorts from the white establishment.

Judge Kovitzky

A older judge of uncompromising disposition, he is assigned to the McCoy case. He is the one official in the criminal justice system who is represented with wholly disinterested motivations.

Quigley

The investigator employed by Thomas Killian on the McCoy case.

Arthur Ruskin

The aged and very wealthy husband of Maria Ruskin. A Jewish man, he has made his fortune running charter flights for Muslims to make pilgimages to Mecca.

Shelly Thomas

The Girl with Brown Lipstick. A young woman on a criminal trial jury in the Bronx, with whom Lawrence Kramer attempts to have an affair.

Major Themes

Universal Cynicism

Tom Wolfe's version of New York in *Bonfire of the Vanities* displays the worst of human nature, and very little of the good. In Wolfe's New York, venal self–interest motivates everyone but the suckers, ethnic and racial bigotry is extreme (and often justified), and the only character who is presented entirely without flaws is the six–year–old Campbell McCoy. Men use women for little other than sexual gratification, and women use men almost entirely for monetary or social gain.

Not unlike Dickens, Wolfe directs much of his cynicism at institutions -- particularly the criminal justice system. The prosecution of "The Great White Defendant" by the politically–motivated District Attorney Weiss, out of all proportion to the severity of the crime, and particularly the manipulation of truth and justice by the news media, show Wolfe's cynical view of these flawed apparatuses of human society. The skewering of the McCoy's gilded Park Avenue world is particularly severe. Those in power fail to represent the disinterested abstractions (justice, civil rights, etc.) that they ostensibly represent, and that's the understatement of the decade.

Childishness in the Adult Male

Wolfe has two of his main characters -- Sherman McCoy and Lawrence Kramer -- repeatedly questioning the entire world they have built for themselves. When Sherman's world is shaken by the threat of his arrest he vacillates between wishing he had given up his materialist high–society rat race life in New York and moved to Tennessee, and trying to salvage that same New York life. Lawrence Kramer, through his fantasies and pursuit of Shelly Thomas, seeks to escape his life of prosecuting and feeding "the chow" (black and Latino defendants) into the criminal justice system in the Bronx.

Each of these men have chosen and pursued their professions, and have likewise married and had a child, but they each fight against the families and lives they have created. Each of them lack the maturity to accept the responsibilities of husband and father, and seek to "cheat" on that life through fantasy and infidelity. Each of them is intelligent enough to know the imperfection of their lives -- Sherman knows that the Park Avenue obsession with wealth and its trappings masks a soulless existence, and Lawrence understands that the criminal justice system he serves is often very unfair, and he is doomed to a life of middle–class struggling in Manhattan, but neither of them have the maturity or courage to break out of their lives to make something different for themselves.

And through this lack of moral strength they betray their wives, and vacillate between trying to justify their existence within their flawed worlds, and fantasizing their way out of them. This kind of behavior is paralleled almost directly between the two men, albeit on different social levels. Each of them lives beyond their means, and balms his ego with an affair. Their moral failures are merely symptoms of their shared diseases -- cowardice and apathy, coupled with ambition, avarice, selfishness and childishness.

Animalism

In almost every reference to sex or sexually attractive people, Wolfe uses the term "animal." When Sherman sees an attractive young woman on the street he composes a mental text for the two of them in which they each describe themselves as "frisky young animals." For Wolfe, the idea of sex is so bound up with the idea of physicality that it reduces human beings to animals.

The animal metaphor continues in the "jungle" description of the Bronx. The criminals and residents of the Bronx are frightening and foreign creatures to the Manhattanites Sherman and Maria, and they react towards the two young men, Roland and Henry, in a wholly defensive way, as one would react to an approaching predatory animal. When Sherman is "victorious" in this confrontation he is "King of the Jungle" -- a metaphor which conjures up the idea of a lion.

Indeed, animal imagery abound in the novel. The lion metaphor is repeated in reference to Sherman's father, John McCoy, the "lion" -- a great and powerful lawyer -- of his firm Dunning, Sponget, and Leach. Fallow and his cronies at Leicester's call the Americans they dupe into buying their drinks "fish." Most tellingly, Sherman refers to his "animal self" when he tells the lie to Judge Kovitzky about the origin of the tape of he and Maria talking about the accident. Wolfe makes it clear that the animal self is underneath all the vanity and superficial glamor of the Park Avenue life Sherman McCoy leads.

The McCoy case as a morality play

The Sherman McCoy case, though a simple hit–and–run in court, grows into a flash point for the culture war of the eighties. The press and even the district attorney's office take prosecution McCoy to be a way to symbolically right the racial wrongs of the entire city of New York. Even Peter Fallow and Gerald Steiner discuss it as a morality play for the sensationalist press. The people involved in it -- Sherman McCoy, Henry Lamb, Mrs. Lamb, Reverend Bacon -- become symbols rather than human beings.

Though DA Abe Weiss says that he would like to treat every case individually, he admits that the case load in the Bronx makes that impossible. And when the Great White Defendant (Sherman McCoy) becomes available, Weiss, ADA Kramer, Reverend Bacon, and the press cannot resist treating the case as a means to tear at the white W.A.S.P. power structure that controls Manhattan. It becomes irrelevant whether Sherman is innocent or not -- he is a white defendant in a case of a black victim in the Bronx. The press and criminal justice system seem to find this inversion of power to be a juicy opportunity to avenge the social injustice in New York. The whole affair ultimately is not about Sherman McCoy versus the system, or even Sherman McCoy against Henry Lamb, Mrs. Lamb, and Reverend Bacon. It becomes Park Avenue versus the Bronx.

Subplots

There are several interesting and entertaining subplots aside from the main plot of *Bonfire of the Vanities* which serve little perceivable purpose to the main action of the story. The reason they are used are merely to add atmosphere, explicate characters, relieve the tension of the racially–charged main plot line, and allow for satire.

An example is the subplot of Lawrence Kramer's attempted affair with Shelly Thomas. His infidelity adds or detracts nothing from the plot, but simply shows what kind of a man Lawrence Kramer is. He's much like Sherman, egotistical and self–delusional, and able to justify his own immoral actions by his childish arrogance. The final entry into this subplot, in which Larry attempts to use Maria Ruskin's illegal sublet as a trysting place for Shelly Thomas and himself, is a wry comic comment on the flawed nature of the criminal justice system in New York.

Similarly, the subplot of Reverend Bacon's appropriation of the Episcopal Diocese of New York's $350,000 for himself rather than the construction of a day care center only illustrates the Reverend Mr. Bacon's moral turpitude and his method of exploiting the racial inequalities in New York.

1980s Excess

Tom Wolfe ruthlessly exposes the superficiality of 1980s culture. His criticism is not only confined to the very rich, the materialism of middle–class people is derided, too. Larry Kramer and his wife, for example, attempt to maintain an expensive Manhattan apartment for the sake of status. Kramer also lives beyond his means as he pursues his affair with Shelly, taking her to absurdly expensive restaurants just to seem as though he belongs.

Wolfe directs his most serious criticism, however, to the very rich, with their extravagant dinner parties, 6–block hired–car rides which cost $250, and thousand–dollar flower arrangements. The restaurant industry in particular gets sharp criticism. La Boue D'Argent, one of the fanciest restaurants in town, translated means either "The Silver Mud" or "Mud Money." It doesn't mean "the silver boar" as the large statue in the entrance implies. When Arthur Ruskin collapses dead in their restaurant, they show absolutely no concern. With Ruskin dead, he can no longer pay for their services; thus, why should they care about him?

Reverend Bacon, though ostensibly concerned with the construction of the Little Shepherd Day Care Center and other much–needed social programs in Harlem, is shown in clothing almost as expensive as Sherman McCoy's and living in a mansion. He is, perhaps, the worst example of "vanity," for his mission is purported to be charitable rather than selfish.

Hypocrisy

Hypocrisy is rife in this novel, and most evident in the two leaders depicted on opposing sides, Reverend Bacon and the Mayor of New York. Neither of these men are truly concerned with the people of New York, but rather with their own advancement and profit. Each, in his way, is racist, but decries racism at every turn. Each purports to be "of the people" but uses his position of power for monetary gain.

The hypocrisy and pretension of American life is everywhere in *Bonfire of the Vanities*. Peter Fallow, especially, practices such deception that his journalism can hardly be called non–fiction. Larry Kramer is so concerned with his masculinity that he exhibits bravado in court to impress a pretty juror, and has such a self–hatred of his own Jewishness that he affects the toughness of an Irish cop.

The rich, especially the McCoys, the Bavardages, and the Ruskins, are rapacious and superficial in the extreme, and try to insulate themselves from the social injustice and race strife in their city as much as possible. Very few characters, even the innocents like Edward Fiske, are without the stain of pretension and ego. This focus on hypocrisy sharpens the satire of the novel.

Class and language

In the novel, Tom Wolfe carefully tailors his dialog to mimic real speech among New Yorkers of every class. He painstakingly records accents in words, such as Maria's "Shuhmun" and the affected bad grammar, such as "They ain't," of Larry Kramer and the detectives. The African–American and Jewish New York patterns of speech are reproduced, including vocabulary, syntax, and accents. With the high–society crowd, Wolfe peppers his prose with fashionable phrases, especially in French and German, and Briticisms. He realistically recreates the varied forms of English spoken in New York in the 1980s.

Glossary of Terms

Arraign

To call or bring before a court to answer to an indictment.

Arrant

Downright; thorough; unmitigated; notorious.

Bergere

A chair of the 18th century, having arms with closed spaces between them and the seat

Blasted heath

A Shakespearean reference -- the land the witches appeared on was a "blasted heath." A heath, in British English, is any area of uncultivated ground. "Blasted" means damaged -- such as what might happen to a battlefield. The blasted heath in *Bonfire of the Vanities* surrounds the Edgar Allen Poe Towers where the Lamb family lives. It illustrates the dismal public housing in the Bronx.

Cabal

A small group of secret plotters, as against a government or person in authority.

Comme il faut

French phrase meaning "as it is necessary".

Diffident

Lacking confidence in one's own ability, worth, or fitness; timid; shy. Restrained or reserved in manner or conduct.

Entre nous

A French phrase meaning "between us", meant to convey confidentiality.

Fatuous

Foolish or inane, especially in an unconscious, complacent manner; silly.

Fauteuil

A French upholstered armchair, especially one with open sides.

Homunculus

A diminutive human being.

Indict

To bring a formal accusation against, as a means of bringing to trial, usually with a grand jury.

Logorrhea

Pathologically incoherent, repetitious speech.

Incessant or compulsive talkativeness; wearisome volubility.

Lovat

A grayish blend of colors, especially of green, used in textiles, as for plaids.

Obiter dicta

Law: an incidental or supplementary opinion by a judge in deciding a case, upon a matter not essential to the decision, and therefore not binding as precedent.

Orotundity

Characterized by strength, fullness, richness, and clearness. Of a style of speaking: pompous or bombastic

Paillard

A slice of veal, chicken, or beef that is pounded until very thin and cooked quickly.

Prole

A member of the proletariat. A person who performs routine tasks in a society.

Raconteur

A person who is skilled in relating stories and anecdotes interestingly

Saturnine

Sluggish in temperament; gloomy; taciturn.

Solecism

A nonstandard or ungrammatical usage, as "unflammable" and "they was." A breach of good manners or etiquette.

Any error, impropriety, or inconsistency.

Sylvan

Consisting of or abounding in woods or trees; wooded.

Tachycardia

A rapid heart rate, especially one above 100 beats per minute in an adult.

Tambour door

A flexible shutter used as a desk top or in place of a door, composed of a number of closely set wood strips attached to a piece of cloth, the whole sliding in grooves along the sides or at the top and bottom.

Teleology

The doctrine that final causes exist. The study of the evidences of design or purpose in nature.

Torpor

Sluggish inactivity or inertia. Lethargic indifference; apathy.

Tout le monde

A fashionable French phrase meaning "all the world", or "everybody."

Turnvereiner

A German term, originally meaning a person who practices gymnastics. Sherman uses it to describe Freddy Button, an excessive smoker, as a "nicotine *Turnvereiner.*"

W.A.S.P.

Acronym for White Anglo–Saxon Protestant. This is the ethnicity which held, or seemed to hold, much of the power in late 20th–century New York. The New York City region, according to Wolfe's novel, was much more concerned with the snobbery and imitation of this ethnic group than the rest of the country. Sherman McCoy is a WASP. It generally applies to old–money Ivy–League–educated families.

Short Summary

The Bonfire of the Vanities, set in New York City in the nineteen eighties, has as its protagonist Sherman McCoy, a self–dubbed "Master of the Universe." McCoy makes a million dollars per annum on Wall Street. He is married to Judy McCoy, and they live with their six–year–old daughter on Park Avenue while maintaining a weekend house in Southampton, Long Island. Much of the action of the story takes place in the extremely decadent world of Park Avenue in the 1980s. Sherman and Judy McCoy's life of elegant apartments, profligate spending, and shallow friendship plays out amid Sheraton furnishings, marble floors, and $2000 suits.

Behind his wife's back, McCoy is conducting an affair with a younger woman, Maria, the socialite wife of another Park Avenue millionaire. One night, after picking her up from the airport, they make a wrong turn into the Bronx. There they have an encounter with a pair of young African–American men; this encounter possibly results in an accident that leaves one of the African–American men dead. McCoy and his mistress flee the scene, resolved not to tell anyone, including the police. At the time of the "accident," Maria was driving Sherman's car.

An unscrupulous civil attorney, Albert Vogel, finds out about this incident, including the information that the driver of the car was probably white, and feeds this news to Peter Fallow, a tippling British reporter at the New York daily newspaper *The City Light*. Fallow distorts the facts of the story to such an extent that certain African–American groups, led by the extortionist Reverend Bacon, take the story up as a rallying point against racial injustice. The story becomes politically charged and Bacon leads an effort to bring the perpetrators to justice.

Meanwhile, Abe Weiss, the District Attorney in the Bronx, is up for re–election. The same Reverend Bacon has been vocally opposed to his campaign, accusing him of favoring white interests. Desperate for African–American votes, the D.A. ruthlessly prosecutes Sherman McCoy. Meanwhile, his Assistant District Attorney assigned to the case, Larry Kramer, wrestles with serious self–esteem issues. Kramer uses the high profile of the case to attempt to impress his would–be mistress, Shelly Thomas.

Sherman ends up indicted for the crime after his mistress Maria and the other witnesses lie to legal authorities. Sherman uses the services of a flamboyant and street–wise Irish–American lawyer, Tommy Killian, who knows the criminal justice system inside and out. Though Sherman gets off through a trick involving a fraudulent taped conversation, he is not free of legal woes. All his assets are appropriated or frozen, and his wife and child leave him. He fights against the legal and political system that ruined him, and grows into a vocal critic of society.

Throughout the novel, Wolfe writes in a bitingly satiric style, sparing no one from the top to the bottom of society. The Mayor of New York, the Reverend Bacon, the D.A., prosecutors, middle–class people, the police, and the poor minorities of

Harlem and the Bronx are all shown to be selfish and morally flawed. The wealthy W.A.S.P. world of Sherman McCoy, however, with its Park Avenue shindigs and its pandering to artists–of–the–moment, is shown to be the worst bastion of elitism, prejudice, and self–delusion.

Summary and Analysis of Prologue - "Mutt on Fire" and Chapter 1 - "The Master of the Universe"

Summary

In the Prologue, the Mayor of New York, a Jewish man up for re–election soon, gives a speech in a Harlem neighborhood. His predominantly black audience heckles him and calls him ethnic epithets. The Mayor attempts to quell the restless crowd with a litany of the things he has done for Harlem and the black community, but the crowd is having none of it. In his thoughts he upbraids the angry African–American crowd as insolent. He thinks that they have been hoodwinked by the inflammatory Harlem religious and social leader Reverend Bacon. He reflects on the Reverend Bacon's underhanded and fraudulent activities. The mayor's thoughts also turn to Sheldon, his assistant, who was supposed to lace the crowd with his supporters.

The mob becomes violent and begins to throw things at the Mayor, including a half–empty bottle of mayonnaise. At last, the Mayor gives up trying to make his speech and decides to leave. A henchman of Reverend Bacon, a tall man wearing a gold earring, calls the Mayor a particularly insulting name as the Mayor is attempting to leave. The Mayor is shuffled down a stairway and leaves the building safely, but not before one of his bodyguards elbows the man in the solar plexus.

In Chapter One, we meet Sherman McCoy (who has dubbed himself a "Master of the Universe) in his sumptuous Park Avenue apartment. We learn of his family structure (wife Judy, six–year–old daughter Campbell, servants, dachshund Marshall) and his wealth. His wife, though pretty, is forty years old, two years Sherman's senior. McCoy fancies himself to be "aristocratic": the epitome of a New York Ivy League W.A.S.P. He works in the richest bond market in history, from which he earns an obscenely large salary. He thinks of his wife, the daughter of a Midwestern history professor and not a Knickerbocker (a term for an old Anglo–Saxon New York family) like him, as socially inferior, and he is particularly disdainful of her efforts to become a decorator. He sneers at the over–lavish way she has fitted out their Park Avenue apartment. For these faults –– and her age –– Sherman sees fit to have a mistress.

Sherman takes Marshall for a walk so that he can slip away from his domestic life for a few minutes to see his mistress Maria in her "hideaway" – an illegally sublet apartment a few blocks away. Out on the street, Sherman dials a number in a phone booth, thinking that he has called Maria. By mistake, he dials his own home number. He does not recognize his own wife's voice and asks for Maria. Judy knows that it's him, but Sherman hangs up without answering her. He calls again and reaches Maria in her hideaway and arranges to meet her.

In the apartment, Maria shows him a new painting she has obtained by the of–the–moment artist Filippo Chirazzi. She counsels Sherman not to lie to his wife about the phone call; Maria herself is perfectly open about her affairs with her husband.

After their rendez–vous, Sherman goes home to a confrontation with his wife. He continues to deny that he called and asked for Maria. His wife says that he is cheap and a liar, and inwardly he agrees with her. At the end of the chapter, Sherman turns on the television and sees the riot in Harlem at the Mayor's speech.

Analysis

The Prologue, which introduces the relatively minor character of the Mayor, and the important character of Reverend Bacon, presents the novel's background of inflamed race relations. This setting immediately contrasts with Sherman McCoy's insular, high–status world. McCoy does not worry about race –– he is preoccupied by his obsessions with sex, money and status. His domestic drama seems to be untouched by the discontent brewing in Harlem –– only brief run–ins with the "street punks" and "breaking news" on the television bring out his racial consciousness. The "street punk" run–in is especially telling, as the man McCoy takes to be a black vagrant is in fact a white man; in a glimpse we see the fear of African Americans buried within McCoy, and his eagerness to avoid the subject at all costs. As a rich, pedigreed white man –– a Master of the Universe –– McCoy is priviledged not to have to think about race. More precisely, he does not yet have to acknowledge that his power and prestige follows from his race, not his abilities. Not yet, anyway.

The rest of the city tells another story. Jews, Irish, Italians, Blacks, Hispanics –– all races and ethnicities are constantly aware of one another. They seem to interact only prejudicially, assuming that the worst stereotypes about every other group must be true. Wolfe presents us with a poisonous atmosphere, fueled by discontent and social injustice (of which W.A.S.P.s like McCoy enjoy the advantage) and manipulated by shrewd and power–hungry provocateurs like the Mayor and, above all, Reverend Bacon.

To turn to the women in the book, they come off no better than the men. Maria Ruskin, with her dismissive attitude toward adultery, seems as capable of betraying Sherman as she does her own husband. (Maria's last name, incidentaly, is the same as a British art critic of the 19th century –– perhaps an offhand reference to her fascination with the work and person of painter Filippo Chirazzi.) Likewise, Judy McCoy, though more sympathetic than Maria, is mocked for her wholesale buy–in to the Park Avenue "social X–ray"–style wife. She is assiduously thin and affected. Perhaps she is a nice woman ineptly playing the Park Avenue socialite in an attempt to keep her horrible husband happy –– like Maria, we never really get to know Judy.

The comic description of Sherman, struggling with the dog in the rain and bumbling his efforts at adultery, are meant partly for laughs but also to show his essential innocence. Sherman, despite his opinion of himself as a master of the world, has never really known life. He clings to outdated notions of class, social, ethnic, and educational privilege. He is moral in a sort of abstract way, in that his major scruples (other than fidelity to his wife – and this he tries to rationalize away through his high status and financial success, and his wife's age) have never been challenged. He still harbors romantic notions about his mistress, and suffers guilt for his infidelity. He, like Peter Fallow will say later in the novel, is a childish American, without any insight into the social upheaval simmering around him.

Summary and Analysis of Chapter 2 - "Gibraltar" and Chapter 3 - "From the Fiftieth Floor"

Summary

In Chapter Two we meet Lawrence Kramer, an Assistant District Attorney in the Homicide Division of the Bronx. He is married to Rhoda Kramer, a red–haired Jewish woman, and they have a new baby son, Joshua, whose English nurse is payed for by Rhoda's mother. They live in a three–and–a–half room apartment on the Upper West Side, which is an expensive but not particularly large Manhattan living space. It becomes clear during Larry's morning routine that the English nurse looks down her nose at these Jewish Americans in their tiny apartment. On the whole, Larry's self–esteem is pretty low, for he is worried about money and is depressed that his wife is beginning to look like her mother.

Larry has been dreaming about The Girl with Brown Lipstick, a pretty juror on a case he is prosecuting. Even sleeping in the same bed with his wife, so soon after the birth of their son, Larry has fantasies about other women. He appears, though his morning thoughts, as deluded and egotistical as Sherman McCoy -- albeit on a lower social rung. Like Sherman, he sees about the riot in Harlem on the morning news.

Larry inwardly criticizes his wife for being fat after delivering his child, and for having a New York Jewish accent. He muses that he will no longer be able to work out, because the nurse sleeps on the convertible couch in the living room where he lifts weights. He also moans that they can't afford an au pair, which means that Rhoda will not be able to go back to work. This will make it difficult for them to live in the Upper West Side on his relatively small ADA salary.

Kramer starts off for work, and sees a former Columbia Law School friend of his leave an expensive apartment building and get into an expensive car. This classmate had gone to work at a downtown law firm, and is obviously doing much better financially than he. Kramer feels morally superior for having decided to "make a difference" in the DA's office, rather than work downtown solely for money, but it's obvious that he is also ashamed of his down–market appearance because he avoids seeing his friend.

After his dangerous journey through the subway to the Bronx, Kramer walks toward the Bronx County Building, where he works. It stands, to his mind, like Gibraltar amid the "poor sad Sargasso Sea of the Bronx." He muses on how no one, not even armed guards or tough men like himself, ever leaves the building for lunch. Though they hold the power over the borough and dispense justice to its residents every day, the workers at the Bronx County Building are plainly terrified of the Bronx.

As Kramer nears the building, he and Judge Myron Kovitzky, who is also entering the building, get severely insulted by a gang of prisoners. While Kramer frets and worries that they are talking directly about him, Judge Kovitzky shows his courage and shouts down the prisoners.

In Chapter Three we follow Sherman to his workplace – a very different place from Kramer's Gibraltar in the Bronx. Sherman walks his daughter Campbell to her bus stop, and indulges in admiration of himself and for the "nip of fatherhood" that he takes each morning. He also glories in his privileges, and the way he is able to indulge his daughter in a private school –– where all the Best Families send their daughters. Sherman has an awkward conversation with his daughter about whether or not there is a God. At the bus stop, Sherman takes the opportunity to ogle and fantasize about another child's mother, Mrs. Lueger.

On the way into work, Sherman sees an attractive young woman and he takes a moment to ogle her, also. He takes an expensive taxi into work, reflecting on how his father, even today at the age of 71, on principle still takes the subway. Sherman has no such principles, and enjoys his isolation from the griminess of the city.

At Pierce &Pierce, the investment banking firm for which Sherman works, Ivy–educated men are already screaming into phones and swearing at computer screens. The bond salesmen make most of the money for the firm, and Sherman is the best bond salesman in the firm. Sherman reflects on a huge deal, the Giscard, which he has put together and will soon be bring to a successful transaction, he hopes. It would net him, personally, $1.75 million if he is successful, with which he could pay off his apartment loan. He meets with some associates and his boss, Gene Lopwitz, by telephone from England, inwarldy relishing his power and dismissing his domestic troubles.

Analysis

Wolfe uses neat symmetry in showing us the contrasting morning routines of Lawrence Kramer and Sherman McCoy, who will later be adversaries. Neither man comes off too well.

Larry is self–conscious, egotistical, lacking in self–esteem, and selfish enough to desire an affair with a juror a few weeks after the birth of his first child. He worries constantly about status, about what other people think, and how he can get away with things and "work the system." He flatters himself that he is "making a difference" by working for peanuts in the DA's office rather than working for a large law firm, but he is not happy with his lot, and longs for more money, a different (or perhaps no) wife, and an affair with another woman.

Wolfe suggests that everything one does in New York reflects one's social status. He sets up a series of parallels to make this comparison quite easy. Larry must brave a dangerous subway ride into the Bronx, while Sherman enjoys a comfortable taxi down to Wall Street. Whereas Larry frets ineffectually over the expense of his new child, Sherman drops his beautiful daughter off at an elite private school. Larry dreams of an affair with a beautiful socialite; Sherman has one.

Wolfe even gives us contrasting portraits of the men with their bosses. Larry is mildly humiliated when the Judge he works under is able to shout down the insulting group of prisoners. We see clearly how low Larry is on the chain of command, and how contingent his relative failure is on his lack of guts. Sherman, on the other hand, is jaunty and cocky in his phone meeting with his London boss. He sees no man as his equal -- let alone his superior -- and impatiently awaits the day when his status will be equal to his self–concept.

The men are very similar -- sex–obsessed, money–obsessed, status–obsessed, and lacking in insight about themselves and others -- with only one major difference: whereas Sherman is for the most part content, Larry is discontent. This difference, despite their commonalities, is enough to make the men grave enemies.

Summary and Analysis of Chapter 4 - "King of the Jungle" and Chapter 5 - "The Girl with Brown Lipstick"

Summary

Sherman takes his expensive Mercedes two–seater to the airport to pick up his mistress, Maria Ruskin. He has been on "model behavior" at home for a week now, and his wife's frostiness following the phone mishap has abated somewhat. He retrieves the glamorously dressed Maria and helps her and her prodigious amount of luggage into the car.

During the drive, Maria distracts him with talk of a British man on the plane who had been flirting with her. He had mentioned the 16th–century poet and playwright Christopher Marlowe and Maria does not know who Marlowe was. Sherman condescendingly lectures about Marlowe, and the two get into a mild argument. This causes him to miss his turn and end up in the Bronx rather than in Manhattan.

The couple struggle to find their way out of the Bronx, where they are conspicuous white people in an expensive car. Just as they have almost reached the George Washington Bridge back to Manhattan, they are stopped by a tire in the road. Sherman gets out to move it and two young black men come toward him, saying "Yo! Need some help?" Sherman and Maria panic, automatically assuming that the men are there to rob them. Sherman throws the tire at the larger man, and Maria gets into the driver seat. Sherman runs back into the car, knocking over the skinny man on his way. The man falls up against the back fender of the car, and Maria grazes him as she speeds away.

As they drive away, Sherman and Maria discuss frantically what may have happened. Sherman is sure that they have hit one of the men; Maria seems unconcerned by this. They reach her "hideaway" apartment and talk the situation over. Sherman wants to go directly to the police, but Maria is vehemently against this. She argues that they don't know what happened, that it would be awkward for them to be caught publicly together, and that, after all, she was the one driving -- not Sherman. He worries that the boys were offering help, but then Maria strokes his ego, telling him that he was "King of the Jungle," defending them from the dangerous young men of the Bronx. They congratulate themselves on their escape.

Sherman leaves the hideaway and brings his car back to the garage where he keeps it with his other car, a Mercury station wagon. He is confronted by Dan, the garage attendant, whom Sherman dislikes for being so familiar. The attendant notices that Sherman's jacket is torn. The victorious Sherman struts home feeling like a real man.

In Chapter 5, we find Larry in his office. We meet his officemates, Andriutti and Caughey, who are also ADAs. They discuss their boss Abe Weiss, and his fascination with the news media. Their nickname for him is "Captain Ahab" because he is on the lookout for the Great White Defendant –– a white man whom the DA office could prosecute. Since the vast majority of the people who Larry and his associates prosecute are black or hispanic, and since Weiss is up for re–election, the DA's office is eager to show that their execution of justice is even–handed and colorblind. The ADA's agree: for once, they would like to prosecute someone who isn't an oppressed minority.

Larry ponders the nature of his job, and indulges in a little self–congratulation of the fact that he is the rare Jewish man in the Homicide Bureau. For many years it had been almost exclusively Irish, and, though he doesn't easily admit it, Larry would much rather be Irish than Jewish. While Larry and his friends talk, the first information about the McCoy case comes in. Henry Lamb, the young man that Maria clipped in the Bronx, is near–death in a hospital. He says that he was hit by a Mercedes–Benz.

Larry goes off to prosecute the case against Herbert 92X, a African–American Muslim on trial for manslaughter. We learn that such cases are so plentiful in the Bronx that hardly any cases receive individual attention. A judge's effectiveness is almost entirely determined by how many cases he can get through, which encourages plea bargaining and discourages jury trials. The sad story of Herbert 92Xs trial is told – how he was driving a truck which was hijacked. The hijackers realized they had hijacked a truck of their own employers, so they went back to find Herbert 92X (who has adopted 92X as his Muslim name, like Malcolm X). When they found him, Herbert thought they were coming back to kill him, so he fired his gun at them. He missed and killed an innocent bystander. Herbert reads from the Koran at the trial and protests his innocense. Larry pulls out all the stops on this trial to impress the girl with brown lipstick, Shelly Thomas, who is on the jury.

Later, back in the office, Larry gets a call from Detective Martin about the Henry Lamb case. He rushes to Lincoln Hospital to interview the mother of the injured young man, as Henry has fallen into a coma.

Analysis

Chapter 4 contains Maria's and Sherman's account of the accident that occurred in the Bronx. Wolfe emphasizes the tragiccomic nature of this event, which was very preventable. The death would have been avoided if Sherman had not agreed to pick up Maria at the airport, or if Sherman had conducted an affair at all, or if Maria had not had a secret "hideaway" that allowed her to come home a day early and deceive her husband, or if they had not had the disagreement in the car about Christopher Marlowe.... The event is arbitrary and accidental, yet, as we will see, it sets off the seething tensions in New York that are neither arbitrary nor accidental, namely, the pervasive realities of –– and manipulations of –– racial and social injustice. The fact that such a senseless, tragic event could be eventually imbued with such widespread significance illustrates the precariousness of New York City politics.

To complicate things further, the event is highly ambiguous. Later, Roland Auburn (the larger young man), Maria, Sherman and others will all give quite divergent accounts of the events. Wolfe is careful to capture the confusion and ambiguity of the event right away. Each character experiences reality through his or her own adreneline–charged point–of–view, and each is determined to retell events in the best light possible. Even from the outset we see Maria and Sherman rationalizing and rethinking the accident to make themselves look better. Soon, this process will be carried to its extreme in the court of law.

Chapter 5 provides background on the criminal justice system in the Bronx, a world of difficult–to–prove cases, pointless violence, and eternal backlogging of justice. Cynicism reigns among the ADAs, who know that there is little hope of change in the Bronx. They dream of prosecuting white people not out of a sense of justice, but just to quiet their own (white) consciences a little bit. The ADA's are also very sensitive to the role of the media in "justice," and their boss' obsession with television and his media image. Thus the Bronx criminal system is shown to be a hollow, cynical approximation of justice performed by an underpaid and overworked staff.

The juxtaposition of the two chapters –– as with Chapters Two and Three –– continues to emphasize the difference between Sherman's world and Larry's. Also, the (ambiguously) criminal event in Chapter 4 is immediately followed by the description of the punishment for such actions in Chapter 5. We are given a not–too–subtle hint that Sherman will be prosecuted in the Bronx for his involvement in the accident on the ramp near Bruckner Boulevard. The foreshadowing is pretty clear: Sherman is obviously flustered when he drops off his car at the garage, and Dan the garage attendant can't help but notice his ripped jacket. Of course such details will play out in the court.

Wolfe leaves intentionally ambiguous the motivation of the young men on the ramp in the Bronx. Was Roland Auburn trying to rob Maria and Sherman? Was the sentence, "Yo! You need help?" an offer of help, as Sherman later thinks, or a threat, as Maria thinks. Wolfe is careful not to sentimentalize the event –– i.e. to make the young men too obviously innocent. It's ultimately not significant to Wolfe whether they had good or bad intentions; what matters is that the worlds of rich white Manhattan and poor black Bronx have collided. Like the first shot fired in a war, this point of contact is ambiguous and open to interpretation, but what ultimately counts is the war to follow. To switch metaphors, Wolfe is more interested in the powder keg than the spark.

Summary and Analysis of Chapter 6 – "A Leader of the People" and Chapter 7 – "Catching the Fish"

Summary

As Chapter 6 opens, we see Sherman at work at Pierce and Pierce, worrying about money and the accident. He is unable to focus, and he retreats to the bathroom to read *The City Light*. He finds no mention of the accident and calms down somewhat.

In this chapter we learn that though Sherman is wealthy indeed, making nearly one million dollars (before taxes) per year, he still lives beyond his means. His apartment on Park Avenue was bought with a personal loan of $1.8 million, which cannot even be refinanced for the equity because "good" Park Avenue building cooperatives refuse to allow tenants to mortgage their apartments. Thus Sherman must complete the "print" (the completed transaction) of the Giscard deal to earn his bonus and pay off the personal loan. McCoy must pay $21,000 a month for the apartment, on top of extravagent daily expenses. And because Judy does not come from a wealthy family, the entire burden of this lifestyle falls on Sherman. Thus Sherman's guilt about the accident, which is affecting his job performance, compromises his entire high–status lifestyle.

Enter Edward Fiske III, a young, white, Ivy League man employed by the Episcopal Diocese of New York to handle business matters. He is in the office of Reverend Bacon (he struggles with the fact that Bacon prefers "Reverend" and not the grammatically correct "the Reverend Mr") in Harlem. Reverend Bacon has accepted $350,000 from the diocese for the construction of the Little Shepherd Day Care Center. Fiske is employed to find out how those funds have been spent, and Reverend Bacon is obstructing his efforts.

We learn that Reverend Bacon is the head of many "charitable" or "non–profit" organizations, such as the Day Care Center, the All People's Solidarity, The Open Gates Employment Coalition.... He has staffed the boards of these organizations with his cronies, many of whom are recently out of prison or still actually in prison. Fiske tries to find out from Bacon what happened to the $350,000, but the Reverend says that it's been used to reserve contractors for the Day Care Center, even though nothing has been built yet. In the background, the recorded voice of the Reverend's deceased mother, Adela Bacon, rises from a phonograph upstairs. We learn that the late Adela Bacon, a gospel recording artist, was a social activist and church leader in her day, and that she ordained her son by her authority alone.

While Fiske is in Bacon's office, Mrs. Annie Lamb, the mother of Harold Lamb, calls Bacon in hysterics. Media outlets also call Reverend Bacon several times about the riot in Harlem at the mayor's speech. It becomes clear that Bacon is a political operator in addition to his church and charitable duties. He tries to explain to Fiske the concept of "steam control," by which the white power structure placates the angry underclass African–Americans in Harlem by these charitable gifts that Bacon "redistributes" in the way he sees fit. Fiske has no headway in recovering the $350,000 and leaves in confusion.

Chapter 7 introduces Peter Fallow, a British man living in New York and working for *The City Light* newspaper. He awakes from a horrible hangover, as usual, to a ringing telephone. Peter agrees to be in the office soon and attempts to make himself presentable.

Peter, an alcoholic who is in debt to his coworkers and in trouble with his boss, is contemptuous of America, criticizing everything from the texture of American carpets to the rhythms of American speech. We learn that Peter was brought over by Sir Gerald Steiner, the publisher of *The City Light*, on false pretenses. Peter became famous writing exposés of the English upper classes; when he lost contact with an aristocractic girlfriend, and thus lost his "insider's" eye on the elites, he had no stories left. However, these stories had attracted the notice of Steiner, who offered Peter a job.

Fallow takes the subway to a British ex–patriate bar and restaurant in Manhattan, Leicester's. He spots a "fish" –– a sucker whom he might pull into conversation and then leave with the bill for the booze –– who happens to be Edward Fiske III. Fiske is easily reeled in. At the end of the evening, Fallow attempts to reel in another fish, an American magazine editor, to pay for his dinner and a bottle of his preferred French wine, "Vieux Galouches" (which translates to "old galoshes).

Meanwhile, the case of Herbert 92X is in session, and Larry is more than usually energetic in the courtroom, which "cooks Herbert 92X's goose." Of course, Larry is playing to the girl with the brown lipstick all along; that Herbert 92X has to suffer for this theatricality is purely incidental.

Analysis

Sherman's financial situation sets him up as a particularly vulnerable defendant. If his income is interrupted even slightly, his entire lifestyle, and that of his wife and child, will collapse. On top of this, Sherman is haunted by his failure to go to the police immediately following the accident –– which he had wanted to do, but which Maria discouraged. Morally and financially, then, Sherman is in dire straits. The life that had seemed so secure in the earlier chapters appears ready to topple.

Edward Fiske is the perfect young, white, over–privileged idealist –– a man Sherman might have been like ten or fifteen years earlier. He considers himself to be "of the people" because he enjoys the music of the African–American gospel singer, Adela Bacon. Also, Fiske is continually duped by everyone around him. Reverend Bacon plays him like a fiddle, dodging Fiske's every effort to account for the

$350,000. Fallow, too, plays Fiske, spotting the young man right away as someone who enjoys pretending to intellectualism. Fiske enjoys the "art of conversation" with Fallow, and meanwhile Fallow drinks for free.

It's apparent that Bacon is living large off of his "non–profit" money. Bacon's glib explanation of "steam control" confuses Fiske to such an extent it gets Bacon off the hook, but it's clear to the reader that Bacon is less concerned with social justice than he is with his own lifestyle. Bacon deflects criticism by alluding to systematic racism and the impossibility of improving the African American condition within "the system," but Wolfe exposes this explanation as hypocrisy as well. We learn (much later in the novel) that the $350,000 came from an African American bishop, thus complicating Bacon's narrative about the "white power structure."

Of course, a reader might want to criticize Wolfe as much as Bacon on this point. Wolfe, after all, is the mastermind in charge of the plot in the novel. It is fully within his own authorial "structural" powers to show Bacon up as a hypocrite -- and, because Bacon is clearly based on figures of power in the African American community like the Reverend Jesse Jackson, to "prove" their mendacity as well. It becomes clearer as the novel progresses that Wolfe has a specific political message of his own. Whether or not you as a reader agree with this message, it's important to keep an eye on it, and not to swallow the upshots of Wolfe's story whole. (Indeed, Wolfe can be a sort of Fallow–esque fisherman–journalist himself, and I'm sure he'd appreciate a wary reader over a Fiske.)

Speaking of Fallow, his nitpicky criticisms of America, though they can be funny, reveal more about his own sour temperament than they do about his adoptive country. He appears envious of the material wealth of American society, and thus clings to his perceived superiority and wit. Of course, "Fallow" is just what his name says -- barren of everything. He isn't an aristocrat, isn't a rake, isn't a wit, isn't an intellectual. He's a poseur, and a pathetic one at that. Thus he is the bottom man in the series of frauds that we've seen -- Reverend Bacon with his phony charities, Sherman McCoy with his phony sense of superiority (for instance, considering himself a "Knickerbocker" when his family really settled in Tenessee), and Larry Kramer with his phony sense of altruism.

Summary and Analysis of Chapter 8 – "The Case" and Chapter 9 – "Some Brit Named Fallow"

Summary

Back at the Bronx County Building, Kramer and Detectives Martin and Goldberg discuss the Lamb case. There is confusion about what actually happened to the boy: he was treated with a broken wrist the night of the accident, but the following day he fell into a coma. Thus his head trauma went undetected at first. The three think that the case will probably blow over, but they go to Reverend Bacon's office in Harlem to discuss it with the boy's mother.

There the Reverend refers to Henry as a "fine young man." The detectives point out that there is no evidence for a hit–and–run, and that the story is unlikely, but the Reverend insists that they move forward with an investigation.

Annie Lamb arrives and impresses the men with her neat appearance and self–possession. She is not the welfare mom from the projects they were expecting –– she is a hardworking a widow, trying to raise her son and keep him out of trouble. She explains that on the night of the accident, Henry came home with a splint on his wrist. He didn't explain what happened and went to bed. The following morning he could hardly talk, but he said that he was hit by a Mercedes–Benz with a license plate beginning with "RE, RF, RB, or RP."

Kramer tells Mrs. Lamb that there is very little evidence to go on, and that her information is unlikely to lead to a trial. This enrages the Reverend, who implies that the white DA's office will not pursue the case because Henry is poor and black. The men leave, feeling sorry for Mrs. Lamb, but not at all hopeful that the case will amount to anything.

In Chapter 9, Peter Fallow receives a call from the celebrity criminal defense lawyer, Al Vogel, offering to give Fallow a story. Fallow has a horrible hangover, but he's in trouble at work and Vogel is offering him a free meal, so he goes to meet him.

Vogel explains the particulars of the Lamb case, emphasizing the hospital mishap of treating Henry's broken wrist instead of his head trauma. Vogel's attempt to drum–up media interest in the story works, as Fallow is intrigued. He calls the city desk at his paper to get the go–ahead to work on the case.

Back in the Bronx, Larry Kramer, who has been involved with another homicide case involving a man called Pimp, learns that Fallow is inquiring into the Lamb case. He explains the state of the case, and how, with the information the DA's office has now, it will be difficult if not impossible to prosecute.

Nevertheless, Fallow pursues the story. He interviews a teacher from Henry Lamb's school, and encourages the man to say that Henry was an honor student "by the standards of the school" -- which are dismally low. Also, though Henry's only option for college would have been the open-enrollment City College of New York, and though Henry had no specific plans for attending college, Fallow describes Lamb as a "prospective college student." Clearly, Fallow is intent on distorting the Lamb case -- and thus benefitting himself, Vogel, and Bacon, as well as the Lambs.

Analysis

The encounter between the detectives and Kramer and the Reverend Mr. Bacon and Mrs. Annie Lamb is fraught with ulterior motives. Kramer's overriding concern, through the car ride there and the entire meeting, is essentially not to appear too sympathetic or "Jewish" to his idol, the Irish Detective Martin. From Kramer's self-hating perspecive, being "Irish" means being tough, uncompromising, and manly. Kramer, who makes his living by posturing in front of juries and clenching his neck muscles, is obviously worried about his own manliness. So he emulates Martin's stoicism, and in the process comes off as unsympathetic to Reverend Bacon and Mrs. Lamb. This "Irish" stoicism -- this attempt to conquer his own "Jewishness" -- opens Kramer up to accusations of being racist and unfeeling. Thus playing into ethnic stereotypes is presented as a perpetually self-defeating process.

Indeed, nearly everything in the case hinges on racial interpretations. Mrs. Lamb, who is understandably suspicious of the white power structure represented by Larry and the detectives, is easily led along by Reverend Bacon. It's impossible not to feel sorry for Mrs. Lamb and her son, who appears to be an essentially good young man, even as one is wary of the glib manner in which Reverend Bacon equates the case with out-and-out racism. Bacon treats the matter of Lamb's treatment in the hospital, for instance, as clearly racist, though we never learn whether hospital staff were negligent and ignored signs of head trauma or whether they were in the right.

Wolfe emphasizes that such motivating factors are almost always ambiguous -- and almost always irrelevent. It doesn't matter whether Lamb was treated well or poorly in the hospital -- just as it doesn't matter whether Kramer acted tough out of disinterest in the case or out of emulation of the "Irish." What matters is how you tell the story after the fact: how you spin it. Motivation can be *shown* to be clear-cut, even though it almost never is. It's already clear who the masters of media spin are in the story, and they've already begun to constuct a clear and easily digestible account of the scholarly, innocent Lamb (get it?) sacrificed to a racist society.

Fallow, for all of his personal failures, knows the art of spin very well indeed. (One might note in passing that as bad as American tabloids can be, British tabloids are among the most outrageous and irresponsible in the world; Fallow might be a proxy for the sensationalist reportage that goes on across the pond.) Fallow manipulates his readers' racism -- and reveals his own -- by insisting that Lamb be presented as "more" than just another kid in the ghetto. Lamb has to be a college-bound "honor student" in order to merit media attention. Fallow, more than anyone else, weaves the narrative of "rich" "evil" "white" Manhattan versus "poor" "virtuous" "black" Bronx.

This is not just simplistic, it's terribly patronizing, especially to the Lambs, who aren't worthy enough for media consumption without being tagged with such stereotypes. Thus the racist white establishment is shown to be working in tandem with Bacon -- both promote an overstated, "good versus evil" narrative, the one to gain prestige and sell papers, the other to increase power and make fraudulant profits. The Lambs themselves disappear into caricatures of "good black people." At least since *Uncle Tom's Cabin*, such representations of "black virtue" have been the flip–side of the demonizations that we more easily recognize as racist. Lamb can be either "just another street thug," as Sherman and Maria see him on the night of the accident, or an innocent "honor student."

Henry Lamb himself, meanwhile, is just as invisible as ever. Indeed, even as Bacon and Fallow wish to see Lamb as a "noble" innocent sacrificed to a white supremacist society, Henry fades into the background. We never get to know who he was, what he did for fun, why he was where he was. His life -- and his senseless death -- matters only as a cipher for Fallow and Bacon to load up with hokum. This is the true sacrifice of Henry Lamb: to the bizarre allegiance of a bigoted Brit and an opportunist Reverend for the sake of power and money. At least, that's how Wolfe seems to frame things.

Summary and Analysis of Chapter 10 - "Saturday's Saturnine Lunchtime" and Chapter 11 - "The Words on the Floor"

Summary

Sherman, Judy, and Campbell, vacationing at their home in Southampton, Long Island, sit at an outdoor table at their beach club with Sherman's parents, John Campbell and Celeste McCoy ("Sixty–five years old and still beautiful," thinks her son). Sherman, still fretting about the accident and the Giscard deal, gains some relief as he watches his daughter play in the sand in a location he remembers well from his own childhood.

His daughter's friend teases her about what her father does for a living, so Campbell asks Sherman what he does at work; he is hard pressed to answer her. Judy chimes in, likening the profits of a bond salesman to the gathering up of crumbs when a big cake is cut up. The implication is that Sherman, though he makes a lot of money, doesn't make anything himself –– he doesn't produce anything. Campbell cries and in retaliation Sherman mocks Judy's interior decorating business. Celeste and John are very uncomfortable.

Back in Manhattan we join the Kramers. As their last chance to go out before the nurse's four–week tenure is up, Rhoda and Larry go to lunch with friends in SoHo. Larry, consumed with jealousy for his friend, watches for a chance to one–up him or make eyes at his girlfriend. He acts like a macho prosecutor from the tough Bronx, but this backfires and he feels that Rhoda is patronizing him. Larry escapes into fantasies of the Girl with Brown Lipstick.

In Chapter 11, Sherman has regained some of his focus and concentrates on the upcoming Giscard deal. He has managed to stifle his paranoia enough to read the news of the world in the *Times* instead of rushing instantly for the local crime news in *The City Light*.

Looking to close the Giscard deal, Sherman takes an extremely important phone call from France. While on the phone, however, he notices that Felix, the shoeshine man's, paper contains an article about the Henry Lamb accident. Sherman tries to read the article and conduct business simultaneously –– he notices an editorial about "white justice," criticizing the DA's office for failing to pursue the case, and a mention of a Mercedes–Benz with the beginning of his license plate number. Distraught, he slips up on the phone and blows the Giscard deal.

In the Bronx, Kramer reads the negative press about the Lamb case. Fallow's article directly accuses Kramer of dragging his feet and not pursuing the matter properly. DA Weiss is furious and homicide chief Bernie Fitzgibbons instructs Kramer to work harder on the Lamb case.

At *The City Light*, Fallow boasts of his triumphant visit to the Bronx and the interview he had with Annie Lamb. He freely exaggerates to make himself more heroic in the eyes of his colleagues, neglecting to inform them that Al Vogel put him on the story in the first place. (Vogel, by the way, has narrowed down the possible vehicles in the Lamb accident from 2,500 to 124 through a contact at the DMV. Vogel promises Fallow the exclusive on this information if he will continue putting pressure on the DA.)

Meanwhile, Larry Kramer takes Shelly Thomas, the Girl with Brown Lipstick, to dinner at a restaurant he can't really afford. She listens to his egocentric account of his manly career prosecuting violent offenders, and Larry thinks things are going well. The problem remains, however, of where to take her for some time alone. He cannot take her to his apartment, obviously, and she lives with her parent in Riverdale.

In Maria's hideaway, Maria and Sherman discuss the accident. Sherman is as ready as ever to go to the police, but Maria insists that they do nothing. A large Hasidic Jewish man interrupts them and accuses Maria of illegally subletting the hideaway. Sherman tries to appease the man, but Maria violently shouts him down and chases him off, leaving Sherman uneasy about her instinct to face down conflict.

Analysis

Like the McCoys' life in general, their Long Island retreat is superficially idyllic and deeply dysfunctional. Roped off from the less privileged in an exclusive beach resort, Sherman proves once again incapable of relating to his daughter, Judy describes Sherman's career in unflattering terms, and Sherman's awkward and uncommunicative parents suffer through it all. The tension between Judy and Sherman, caused by his foolish phone call, has not abated. Campbell, meanwhile, is confused and happy. Though the child merely wishes for an answer to an innocent question, her parents use her as a conduit for their passive–aggressive bickering.

The pattern that Wolfe has established of comparing Sherman's world of privilege with Larry's world of middle–class discontent continues. We move from lunch with the McCoys to lunch with the Kramers –– and the latter event is no less passive–aggressive. Larry's typical concerns –– with social status, money, and his masculinity –– once again rule the day. His attempt to "sell" his job as macho, followed by a retreat into fantasies about the Girl with Brown Lipstick when this fails, illustrate his impotent, frustrated approach to life in general. Later, when Larry finally has his chance with Shelly, he continues to use her almost therapeutically, balming his ego with lies about his "dangerous" profession. She continues to exist as fantasy –– as utterly absent aside from her prettiness and usefulness for Larry.

Indeed, though Wolfe consistently gives his two–dimensional female characters a "purpose" –– that is, he shows their two–dimensionality as following from the perspective of shallow and mendacious men like Sherman and Larry –– one might wonder about Wolfe's ability to write women characters. Though his men are flawed, at least we are given insight into their desires and anxieties, however childish. Larry's crisis of masculinity and Sherman's anxiety over money and the accident make these characters somewhat understandable almost despite themselves. The women in the novel, however, are given almost no depth. They act either inscrutably –– like Maria's insistence on secrecy and confrontation –– or spitefully –– as in Judy and Rhonda's passive–aggressive prodding of their respective husbands. Perhaps these shallow man–woman relationships are more than an indictment of the shallow men and women in the book; perhaps instead they are a result of Wolfe's lack of interest in developing believable women.

Meanwhile, Fallow continues to reveal the oiliness of his character. Clearly, he is Vogel's pawn –– a set–up man for the big pay–off Vogel expects to receive in a civil suit. Needless to say, he has no interest in reporting facts; he bends and embellishes every detail of the story to help foment racial unrest. He and his editors have a cynical interest in "decrying" New York's racist society, and he enjoys the Lamb story both as an opportunity for a scoop and for sanctimonious posturing.

Wolfe delights in little structural tricks like putting Sherman's personal financial fall in the aptly–named Chapter 11 –– an allusion, of course, to bankruptcy. Such details call attention to the extent to which Wolfe has neatly structured his tale, just as he has carefully named his characters (in a way that suggests Charles Dickens) to expose their personalities and roles in the narrative. Many events in the novel, from the ludicrously important Giscard deal (which can be blown in a single phone call), are driven by unlikely coincidences. Sherman *just happens* to learn about the Lamb case *just* as he can ensure his own financial ruin? Thus the novel can feel "over–structured" at times, as though we are reading a cartoonish embellishment of racial unrest and W.A.S.P. finances (not unlike something that a journalist might write –– not a Fallow, perhaps, but a subtler and smarter specimen of the same breed).

This self–consciousness is part of what makes reading Wolfe so fun –– and somewhat frustrating. Perhaps *Bonfire of the Vanities* is not intended to be taken *too* seriously even as it explores some very serious and very real social anxieties. Perhaps Wolfe intends these coincidences and superficial tricks to reflect the superficiality, self–consciousness and "constructedness" of 1980s New York City. Or both; or neither.

Summary and Analysis of Chapter 12 - "The Last of the Great Smokers" and Chapter 13 - "The Day-Glo Eel"

Summary

The enormity of Sherman's gaffe on the telephone with his Giscard contact becomes apparent when he is offered the purchase of the bonds at $6 million dollar loss. The deal is finished, and Sherman stares down the barrel of an $1.8 million dollar personal loan that he will be unable to pay off. In full panic mode now, Sherman retreats to the bathroom to read more about the accident in *The City Light*. The news, of course, is not good. Fallow has maintained the sensationalist nature of the story, accusing the city of "foot-dragging," and revealing that only 124 vehicles in the city could have been involved in the accident. In desperation, Sherman decides to consult his lawyer, an innocuous, W.A.S.P.-y man in his father's firm named Freddy Button.

Button's nonchalance in the face of Sherman's travails, and his constant smoking, unnerves Sherman. However, Sherman is aching to spill his story, and tells Freddy everything. Freddy suggests that Maria may not corroborate Sherman's story and push the blame onto Sherman instead. Freddy then refers Sherman to Thomas Killian of the firm Dershkin, Bellavita, Fishbein &Schlossel, describing Killian as a shrewd criminal lawyer.

Meanwhile, Sherman misses several important transactions at his firm. In addition, he is caught lying about his whereabouts. He is becoming less and less focused on his job, even though it is absolutely essential to his financial survival, and more and more focused on his overwhelming personal problems.

Chapter 13 finds Kramer and Detectives Goldberg and Martin going to the Edgar Allen Poe housing project where Annie Lamb lives. Reverend Bacon has organized a demonstration to protest the lack of investigation into Henry's accident. Ostensibly, the detectives and Kramer are looking for witnesses to the crime, but Weiss has clearly sent them for political reasons. Kramer, ever enamored with "Irish" masculinity, watches Detective Martin, a small man, face down a large black youth for no reason other than to obtain a good parking space.

The demonstrators gather, and Larry Kramer notes the artificiality of the protest. There are several white demonstrators, and support from a gay and lesbian group. It seems less a spontaneous reaction of the people than a publicity stunt staged for television cameras.

Fallow arrives as well and is also surprised by the phony nature of the protest. The television cameras capture footage of Mrs. Lamb and Reverend Bacon, as well as misleading footage of the protest, making it seem larger and more spontaneous than it really is. The action only kicks in once the cameras are rolling. The insincerity of this “protest” depresses both Fallow and Kramer, though Fallow chalks it up to American childishness rather than social injustice. The renowned television reporter, Robert Corso, arrives, and his appearance seems to be more noteworthy than the demonstration itself.

Sherman, trying to keep up appearances, comes home early to be with his family. After his confession to Freddy Button, who counseled honesty with his wife, Sherman attempts to summon the courage to tell Judy about the accident. He looks to her for a sign of tenderness, but she has become inured to his secrecy and lack of interest in her, and she is less and less interested in what he has to say.

Sherman awkwardly admires a clay bunny that his daughter made at school, touched by his daughter's talent but unconvincing in his "family–man" role. Meanwhile, the television news informs them of the letters on the license plate that correspond to Sherman’s Mercedes–Benz. Sherman jokes lightly about it, and Judy doesn’t respond in any meaningful way, so he decides not to tell her –– primarily out of fear of her reaction to his infidelity.

Analysis

The “Day–Glo Eel” refers to the brightly colored cables snaking out from the television vans to the cameras and microphones used to record the demonstration at the Edgar Allen Poe housing projects. The situation follows the logic of "television" reality –– not "real" reality –– with protesters assembled to be on the news or to further Bacon's political interests. Even Peter Fallow is disgusted by the protest –– and when the oiliest character in a novel criticizes an event's oiliness, that's saying something. Wolfe, a veteran reporter of all kinds of civil unrest in the 1960s and 1970s, knows what a real demonstration expressing the views of a group of people looks like, and he makes it clear that this "protest" is a fake. It's the 1980s version of unrest, performed for cameras and home audiences.

Meanwhile, one of the targets of these mechanizations (though few know it yet) displays the extent to which he is cut off from the gravity of his situation. Sherman clings to his insulated, privileged world like a child to a security blanket. He fails to warn his family of the coming trouble –– both financial and legal –– simply because they won't show him tenderness, as though he isn't the reason for their distance! Of course, Sherman's world was never as stable as he believed it was, and the extent to which his former life of comfort rested on a precarious financial gamble (and despite flammable racial conditions that Sherman never understood) is now quite clear.

Sherman's succession of lawyers represents in microcosm the move from a simpler, W.A.S.P.–dominated world (the world Sherman thought to be reality) to a shrewder, multi–ethnic New York. The anachronistic figure of Freddy Button, "The Last of the Great Smokers," provides a moment of humorous repose amidst all of this drama.

Mr. Buttons (another blatantly Dickensian name, by the way) appears to be a person from another, more innocent time -- or perhaps from a Hollywood movie of the golden age. Buttons contrasts starkly with the actual, effectual lawyer who will handle Sherman's case. Killian, an Irish lawyer in an Italian- and Jewish-named firm, represents everything that Sherman mistrusts. Of course, the fact that Sherman's fate rests in the hands of a man whom -- simply because of his ethnic heritage -- Sherman disparages, is deeply ironic. Sherman's outdated world of Long Beach clubs and "Knickerbockers" won't help him now.

Indeed, Sherman's anachronisms are, in many ways, the root of his dilemma. If Sherman could have relaxed his prejudices anywhere along the way, he could have been saved these difficulties. If he hadn't been bound by misguided chivalry to Maria, and his own personal cowardice, he would have followed his first instinct to report the accident, thus eliminating the cover-up and making things a lot less serious in the eyes of the law. If Sherman could have interacted with the young men in the Bronx without freaking out, the accident likely wouldn't have occurred. Even now, Sherman fails to see the extent to which he rests in a tenuous racial position: he is bait for a hungry city. And as Killian illustrates, only by accepting and engaging with the "new" New York -- the 1980s New York -- and leaving the Old New York Knickerbockers for the history books, will Sherman save his life from total disaster.

Summary and Analysis of Chapter 14 - "I Don't Know How to Lie" and Chapter 15 - "The Masque of the Red Death"

Summary

Sherman's body begins to fail him. Insomnia and nightmares plague his nights while he continues the farce of his everyday life, acting as if nothing has changed. He intermittently longs to confide in and be comforted by his wife, but he dismisses the idea. He walks Campbell to the bus stop as usual, and goes into work while frantically looking for information on the case in all the newspapers.

The City Light has another piece about the accident, entitled "Hit–or–Miss Justice." The article admits the legal difficulty of prosecuting the still–hidden Henry Lamb perpetrator, but calls for the search to continue in the strongest language. Sherman realizes that the case has become a crusade.

Freddy Buttons calls him, and informs him that he's called Tommy Killian. Sherman, frayed at the edges, decides to leave work early (at five o' clock, which is early by his former workaholic standard). He arrives at his apartment and collapses with exhaustion.

Bonita, the housekeeper, awakens him to say that two policemen are waiting downstairs to see him. Sherman panics and leaves the cops waiting while he tries to pull himself together. Detectives Martin and Goldberg don't appear particularly suspicious; they admire the Park Avenue splendor of the apartment. Sherman starts evading their investigative efforts, refusing to answer simple questions, which leads the detectives to look more closely at Sherman's case. Sherman's nerves are compounded by annoyance at the familiar mannerisms of the policemen as they question him -- he feels that they should behave like his inferiors. Thus Sherman McCoy comes off very badly. The detectives finally leave, after Sherman insists on speaking with his lawyer, and head straight to the garage where the Mercedes is kept.

Campbell and Judy come home, and Judy inquires if something is wrong. Sherman frantically tries to reassure her that all's well, and that he just needs to run out to Freddy Button's house for a minute. Judy tries to make him stay, reminding him of their important dinner engagement at the Bavardages' place. Sherman tries again to come clean to Judy, but he can't get the words out, and he flees the apartment. He tries dialing Maria from a payphone, but can't reach her either at her home or at the hideaway. In despair, he returns home to dress for dinner.

In Chapter 15, Sherman and Judy arrive at the Bavardages' apartment, a few blocks away from their own. As was the fashion of the rich of Park Avenue at the time, they hire a car for the evening, which costs nearly $250. Sherman, fully aware that his money is just as jeopardized as his good name, frets bitterly about the enormous amount of money he and his family spend on such extravagances. His bitterness continues at the apartment itself, as contempt for the fashionably thin, affected women and inane men of society smolders within him. Moreover, he is unnerved by casual conversational references to the Lamb affair.

At dinner, he is seated by chance next to Maria Ruskin. He worries that his wife will make the connection between the fateful phone call and his dinner companion. The dinner is obscenely lavish, with expensive wines, food, and flower arrangements. Again, Sherman muses on the amount of money spent, and begins to reflect on the vanity of his circle. He tries to talk discreetly with Maria about the Lamb affair, but she maintains that they have nothing to worry about. He promises to call her the following day.

Aubrey Buffing, a poet with AIDS, makes a long speech at the end of the dinner, alluding to Edgar Allen Poe and his story "The Masque of the Red Death." Buffing proposes that the story's description of a culture of excess dancing on amid a horrible plague suits their 1980s culture vis–a–vis AIDS as well. The speech doesn't make much of an impression on the guests. Sherman and Judy then take their leave: she chatting about how nice the party was; he depressed and drunk.

Analysis

The Dickensian caricatures continue, as Wolfe mocks his characters with hidden jokes –– the word "bavardage", for example, is a French word for incessant prattling –– and plainly insulting names, like the writer Nunnally Voyd (nothing–void), Mrs. Rawthrote (raw–throat, with incessant talking), and Lord Gutt, the corpulent British aristocrat.

The broad hint of the "Masque of the Red Death" reference has more than one meaning. The poet Buffing uses the comparison primarily to draw attention to people's indifference toward the AIDS epidemic despite the material abundance of the 1980s. However, another (and Wolfe seems to suggest, greater) plague is raging as well –– a class–sickness engendered by poverty and racism –– which threatens to swallow up the "offshore boutique" of Manhattan. The wealthy and privileged continue their Masque (or "masked ball," an allusion to the social masks that abount at the Bavardages') unaware of the reckoning to come. Wolfe suggests that, like the aristocrats dancing away in the Poe tale, New York society as a whole (not just Sherman) is deluded, and New York society as a whole will fall. He connects this allusion to the "Masque" with the outside, poverty–plagued boroughs by placing Henry Lamb and his mother in the Edgar Allen Poe Towers housing project in the Bronx (where Poe once lived).

In contrast to the obvious caricatures at the party, Wolfe handles the deterioration of Sherman McCoy believably and subtly. Sherman is a man in shock. He refuses to think about the extent of his trouble –– thus he refuses to see Killian, to discuss the

Lamb accident with his wife -- even as his body (and bodies are always aware of massive trauma before minds catch up) falls apart. To cave in and see the Irish Killian would be to give up the W.A.S.P. fantasy, and Sherman is not ready to do that yet. Nevertheless, Sherman has begun on the road to change. His bitter criticisms of the nonsense and excess at the Bavardages' apartment show that he begins to see the vanity of his own class, even if he cannot yet understand the perspective of other classes. Wolfe seems to suggest that "knowing thyself" is a first important step to knowing others, and Sherman seems capable of empathy yet.

Not to belabor the point, but Wolfe's gift for creating complicated, flawed–yet–redeemable characters seems limited to the men in his story. This seems true even in the peripheral characters. Goldberg and Martin, for instance, exhibit complicated personalities, mixing pride, belligerence, acumen, wit and common sense. The detectives are good at their job -- and they show Sherman, the self–dubbed "Master of the Universe," to be the bumbling child that he is. Judy, by comparison, exists as a foil for her husband -- first as a vessel for her husband's disappointment, and then to reflect his self–hatred. Likewise, Maria is little more than a "Lemon Tart" (the nickname Sherman has for young and desirable women), conforming to the predictable trope of the beautiful woman as selfish and morally bankrupt.

Summary and Analysis of Chapter 16 – "Tawkin Irish" and Chapter 17 – "The Favor Bank"

Summary

As Chapter 16 opens, Detectives Martin and Goldberg are pleased as punch. Sherman's suspicious evasiveness, combined with the testimony of the garage attendant, leads the men to belive that they have found their man in the Lamb case. Not only do they have a solid lead in a media–saturated case, the men are on the verge of hauling in the catch of the decade, The Great White Defendant.

As the DA office talks about this development, Larry Kramer reflects on Irish machismo, a mule–like stubbornness (the Irish call themselves "donkeys") that has become the preferred personality of the department. Kramer believes that the other ethnicities in the department –– African–Americans, Italians, Jews, etc. –– all aspire to be pig–headed and courageous, like the Irish, and he is no exception. Meanwhile, Martin and Goldberg relate their interview with Sherman to Bernie Fitzgibbon, chief of the Homicide Division of the DA's office. They humorously describe Sherman's arrogance and inept evasiveness.

Down on Reade Street, Sherman waits for Thomas Killian in the offices of Dershkin, Bellavita, Fishbein &Schlossel. Under the florescent lighting and surrounding by defendants of all colors and creeds but his own, Sherman is totally uncomfortable. He begins to realize that this world he is now mired in has always existed, and that his power and prestige are meaningless here.

When Sherman meets Killian, he's a bit surprised at the lawyer's extremely dapper appearance. Killian, after clearly stating his fee, points out Sherman's errors one by one. Especially crucial, it seems, is his failure to contact Killian sooner, before the police arrived. They turn to the case, and Killian suggests that Maria will betray Sherman. He wants a signed statement from Maria that she was driving the car, and though Sherman says that he will attempt to get it, he seems still chivalrous (or stupid) enough to put his faith in Maria. Killian, who once worked as an ADA, also impresses upon Sherman his importance to the DA office as a Great White Defendant.

In Chapter 17, DA Abe Weiss meets with his assistants about the Lamb case. Larry Kramer is excited to be in on this important meeting, and tries hard to impress the DA. He feels that he is connected to The Power. Weiss' main concern is improving the DA office's press –– especially the jingle going around that "Weiss Justice is White Justice" –– so while they still lack the evidence to go after Sherman McCoy, Weiss' plan is to bring Sherman's picture to Henry Lamb in the hospital, where Lamb might identify him. Of course, Lamb is in a coma, so the plan isn't a good one. Weiss also takes Kramer to task for his gruff manner with Mrs. Lamb, and Kramer protests that Reverend Bacon twisted his words on that occassion.

On Friday afternoon, Judy and Campbell McCoy and the servants drive out to the weekend house in Long Island, as is their custom, and Sherman stays behind, saying that he has to work late. He tries to locate Maria and cannot, so he consults Killian, who suggests that Maria is preparing to betray him. Sherman continues to resist this possibility, though he's quite distraught. Killian emphasizes how important it is to prove that Maria was behind the wheel. He even suggests that Sherman meet her while wearing a wire. Sherman, ever noble, can't conceive of such a deception, but agrees to try to get her to talk to Killian as soon as possible. Meanwhile, Killian reassures him somewhat by making it clear how connected he is in the DA office (as a former ADA himself). Many in that office owe Killian favors, so Killian has a good chance of getting Sherman special treatment.

Elsewhere, Al Vogel continues to play Peter Fallow for all he's worth. They meet at a "pompous and stiff–necked" Chinese restaurant, where Vogel steers Peter toward a new angle in the story: the supposed negligence of the hospital. Peter shakes off his qualms about playing Vogel's stooge and decides to go ahead with this story.

In Larry Kramer's office, a call comes in from the Legal Aid defense of Roland Auburn. Roland is in custody on drug charges, and says he's willing to give his testimony of the Henry Lamb case in exchange for a lighter sentence. Roland says he was the other man with Henry Lamb the night he was hit by the car.

Analysis

Though he still harbors an aversion to familiarity from non–W.A.S.P.s, it is dawning on Sherman just how much smarter people like Killian are than he. Killian ensures this rude awakening when he makes Sherman's colossal blunder with the police clear. Sherman could have avoided the whole ordeal if he had simply talked to Killian before the cops. Not only this, but Sherman also learns that Killian went to Yale Law School. If an Irish "sharpie" like Killian went to Yale, Sherman thinks, then is there any difference anymore between "us" and "them"? Sherman's naivete on this point may strain credibility –– Sherman couldn't have gone to Yale without knowing that non–W.A.S.P.s were among him –– but it emphasizes Wolfe's (perhaps personally–motivated) point that American higher education has shifted somewhat from emphasizing W.A.S.P. "legacies" to rewarding shrewd "sharpies" of all ethnicities. In short, not only is Killian smarter than he is, he's just as pedigreed too. Sherman thus comes to see the extent of his insularity.

Kramer's sycophantic yes–saying in the DA's office show just what a creature of The Power he is. Full of hatred for his ethnicity and his low–status, Kramer wishes to be a part of something meaningful at any cost. His role as Sherman's doppleganger (double) grows clearer as we learn that he too is living beyond his means, trying to support a mistress (Shelly Thomas). However, as in earlier chapters, the similarities between Sherman and Larry end at the surface. Their personalities are mirror–images. If Sherman is an out–of–control arrogant man who needs to learn his insignificance, Larry is all too aware of his insignificance and needs to learn pride in himself. Wolfe leans heavily on stereotypes (the haughty W.A.S.P. versus the self–loathing Jew) but manages to suggest that masculine pursuits of money, status, women and power can spring from diametrically opposite emotional states.

A similar gift for doubling appears as the detectives relate Sherman's bumbling attempts at prevarication from their own perspective. Sherman, who thought himself so clearly above the two men, is as transparent as tissue paper. He is patently ridiculous in the eyes of a couple of street–wise cops, who thus come off as much more well–adjusted and clear–sighted than the Park Avenue Master of the Universe. While Sherman deserves their every barb, note that Wolfe is able to garner sympathy for Sherman even as he mocks him. Sherman's helpless childishness evokes more pity than scorn in the reader, especially now that it's clear that Sherman is on the way to learning humility.

A third parallel in these chapters involves that of DA Weiss with Reverend Bacon. Both men are skilled manipulators of the media, and are far more interested in favorable public opinion and the attendant glory than they are in the ostensible social causes they represent. The personal similarities between the Jewish District Attorney and the African–American minister are great; they merely operate in different spheres.

Killian's exposition of The Favor Bank, like the earlier explanations of the backlogged Bronx justice system and the search for the Great White Defendant, illustrates the extent to which the legal world opporates according to arbitrary (hardly "just") patterns of favoritism. It's very obvious by now that the justice system obeys power, not any abstract ideal of fairness before the law, but Wolfe hammers the point home in his colorful and broad way.

In Sherman's case, The Great White Defendant priority will trump The Favor Bank, not because The Favor Bank isn't an important part of New York law, but because the political timbre of the hour insists upon prosecuting a white man. Wolfe wishes us to see Sherman as caught in a struggle of competing corruption, and to begin to feel a bit sorry for the guy, scum though he may be. Sherman is Wolfe's Lamb (pardon the pun): a not–so–innocent–but–innocent–enough sacrifice to a ravenous race–baiting media. Whether you wish to agree with Wolfe is, of course, up to you.

Summary and Analysis of Chapter 18 - "Shuhmun" and Chapter 19 - "Donkey Loyalty"

Summary

Roland Auburn, accompanied by his Legal Aid lawyer, Cecil Hayden, tells Larry Kramer his side of the Henry Lamb story in order to get out of a drug charge. Kramer notes Roland's athletic physique and street–wise bearing (we walks with the "pimp roll," a swaggar affected by black youth that Larry believes will undermine Roland's credibility as a witness).

As Roland tells the story, he ran into Henry walking to the Texas Fried Chicken restaurant near Bruckner Boulevard. The two young men were not friends because Henry was kept at home most of the time by his mother and didn't engage in criminal activities. (Roland, on the other hand, has been arrested three times already and has earned the media tag "The Crack King of Evergreen Avenue," one of DA Weiss' inspirations.) Roland says that as they were crossing Bruckner Boulevard, they saw the Mercedes. He recalls that the car was driving along the shoulder when it hit Henry. At first Henry said only his arm was hurt. The car stopped, and Roland asked the driver for help and told him that his friend was hurt. Roland accurately describes Sherman and Maria and says that he heard Maria refer to "Shuh–mun." He says that the white people were scared of him, and the woman got into the driver's seat and drove them both away.

When Roland is shown a picture of Sherman and Judy, he identifies Sherman but says that the woman with Sherman was younger and a "hot ticket."

Roland continues his story, saying he took Henry in a gypsy cab to the hospital. Roland knew the driver, a man called Curly Kale. Roland didn't go in with Henry, but took him to the door of the emergency room, and then left. Roland was afraid of being caught by the police if he stayed with Henry. He didn't know of any injuries aside from the hurt wrist. This information is enough for Kramer to make a deal with Roland's lawyer.

In Chapter 19, the change in fortunes in the case of The Great White Defendant reflects well on Kramer. The DA addresses him directly and calls him by name, now, when before he had only sent information through the Homicide Chief, Bernie Fitzgibbon. When the three meet on Monday, they discuss their evidence and decide that the testimony of Dan the garage attendant and the positive ID from Roland is enough to go on. Bernie worries about the suitability of the witness, and Kramer protests that Roland is a solid witness and that they should go forward.

Meanwhile, the spread in Architectural Digest of the McCoy's apartment has come back to haunt them. DA Weiss spots the pictures and envisions a high–profile and dramatic "Park Avenue arrest" at the McCoy's. His plan is foiled, however, as Thomas Killian has already secured a guarantee from fellow–Irishman Bernie Fitzgibbon that the arrest will be made as quietly as possible. Fitzgibbon respects this request out of "Donkey Loyalty" –– solidarity between the New York Irish. Frustrated by this missed opportunity at media attention, Weiss privately plans to make things as difficult as he can for Sherman following the arrest.

Analysis

With Roland's testimony, Wolfe provides the first major differing account of the accident. The differences are quite stark. Roland provides a different location, Bruckner Boulevard rather than the ramp back onto the freeway; a different account of when Henry was hit; a different account of the offer/request for help, "Yo, you need some help?" versus "My friend needs help"; and a different reason for the car's stopping, in response to hitting Henry rather than to a tire in the road. Note that Roland's account, like the expected false testimony of Maria, places Sherman in the driver's seat at the time of the incident.

Because the original account of the accident is relatively straight–forward, the reader naturally mistrusts Roland's story. He may well be attempting to cover up for his impulse at the time: to rob Sherman and Maria. This possibility gains creedence as Wolfe reveals Sherman's criminal history. Again, Wolfe emphasizes that the actual event does not matter. What matters is how the event is told in court –– that is the only "truth" or "reality" that bears consequence at this point. Right now, things look bad for Sherman.

The Architectural Digest story, which Sherman was opposed to from the start, either due to dignity or haughty superiority or both, has had the exact opposite effect that Judy intended. Whereas she hoped that the story would further her career as a designer and announce to "society" that the McCoy's had arrived, the pictures only serve to illustrate the extent of Sherman's hubris. They work against him, highlighting the extent to which he lived a privileged, out–of–touch life before the Lamb incident brought him to justice. One senses again Wolfe's subtle way of shifting blame to the female characters in the book. Judy's garish bad taste and naive desire for celebrity has put Sherman –– who was against such displays in the first place –– in a tough spot with Weiss and the media. It's telling how our failure to know Judy outside of Sherman's perspective builds sympathy for Sherman. Perhaps if her point–of–view were clearer, and her character more three–dimensional, it would be more difficult to root for her husband.

Larry continues to suffer from his inferiority complex, but he seems to be changing into a more assertive man before our very eyes. The importance attached to the Lamb case, coupled with his relentless desire to impress (and eventually to bed) Shelly Thomas, leads Larry to play the "justice" game more aggressively than we're used to seeing in him. Specifically, he shows no second thoughts about promoting Roland as a credible witness (even though he himself had misgivings about Roland's credibility upon first meeting the youth) and moving full–steam–ahead on the Lamb case. Larry is learning to act out of self–interest, not just out of cringing fear. Again, he seems to be a sort of pivot–point for Sherman in this regard. As Sherman falls, Larry rises; as Sherman grows unsure of himself, Larry grows confident. They're like two children on a see–saw.

Finally, the sketch of Cecil Hayden is a sad commentary on the lack of opportunities (as Wolfe sees things) for black attorneys in New York City. Black defendants, we are told, want white lawyers, not black ones, so even a good, smart lawyer like Hayden has few options. Wolfe thus attempts to show how both blacks and whites manipulate racism for advantages. Roland's preference for a white lawyer is playing the system, just like Reverend Bacon's power and prestige rely upon "proving" that New York is racist to the core and that he is necessary.

Summary and Analysis of Chapter 20 - "Calls from Above" and Chapter 21 - "The Fabulous Koala"

Summary

Sherman, once the golden boy of Pierce &Pierce, has been summoned to his boss's office. Gene Lopwitz, who Sherman considers to be a vulgar man, is a Jewish–American Anglophile. His passion for all things British led him to construct a working fireplace on the fiftieth floor of a modern office tower on Wall Street. This enormous undertaking has given Lopwitz insects bites on a sensitive part of his anatomy: they hitched a ride on some logs and attacked the head of the firm.

Just as the meeting begins, an obese opera singer, Bobby Shafflett, calls Gene, who has lent the star–of–the–moment (who knows from the Bavardages' party) his private jet. Sherman waits while Gene schmoozes. Finally, Gene hangs up and berates Sherman for his poor work performance. Sherman, again feeling the same need for confession that he felt in Freddy Button's office, holds back because of Lopwitz's reputation as a shameless gossip.

Tommy Killian has been frantic to get in contact with Sherman, and while in the meeting with Lopwitz Sherman receives word of Killian on the phone. Sherman walks out of Lopwitz' office to take the call, a disrespectful act that does not bode well at all. On the phone, Killian informs Sherman that he will be arrested the following morning. He tells his client that the arrest will go smoothly, which hardly reassures Sherman, who agrees to meet Killian that afternoon.

Sherman returns to Lopwitz's office and explains the matter. Gene has no sympathy for Sherman and informs him that Sherman must go on a leave of absence immediately. Sherman tries to calculate whether he and his family will be able to survive on the money he has saved. He dreads having to come clean about the situation, especially to his daughter, Campbell.

In Chapter 21, Sherman withdraws $10,000 cash from his bank that, which he will need for bail money. The Bank Secrecy Act requires that banks report cash transactions which exceed $10,000. Sherman feels the extent of his trouble, his imminent fall from grace, and the beginning of his financial straits.

Sherman then goes to his father, John Campbell McCoy, known in his day as the Lion of Dunning, Sponget &Leach. Sherman venerates his father, whom he thinks of more as an allegory for strength and unchanging respectability than as a man. Sherman downplays the more sordid details, calling his relationship with Maria a "flirtation." The elder McCoy is shocked that Sherman confided in Freddy Button before him, and disapproves of his advice to retain Thomas Killian as a lawyer.

Nevertheless, he promises Sherman parental support. He asks how Judy is holding up and is aghast that Sherman hasn't told her yet.

At home, Sherman brings Judy into the library with every intention of disclosing the incident, but he tries to hide the seriousness of his affair with Maria, which Judy calls him out on. Sherman has lost all credibility in her eyes, between his long–standing deceptiveness and his failure to be honest even on the eve of his arrest. Judy shows no sympathy.

Sherman then enters Campbell's perfectly furnished room. Oblivious to her luxuriant surroundings, Campbell reads Sherman a book she made starring a koala who comes to New York and jumps into a window to avoid a dog; the koala thus sets off a burglar alarm, summoning police cars. Sherman reads this tale as a premonition of his arrest. He then turns to the coming arrest. Sherman explains that people are out to hurt him and she mustn't believe the bad things they say about him. Campbell embraces her father and tells him that she loves him, and at that moment Sherman feels that Campbell's innocence is lost.

Analysis

In Gene Lopwitz, Wolfe presents another caricature whose manias (Anglophilia, jogging, homey office furnishings, celebrities) capture the insular pettiness of the Wall Street elite. He serves to remind Sherman once again that he is not an irreplacable "Master of the Universe," but merely a cog in the machine. Gene has no qualms about letting him go to the wolves.

Despite Killian's assurances that things will go smoothly –– based largely on his faith in The Favor Bank –– these chapters read as a litany of the things Sherman is set up to lose. Of course the episode with Lopwitz shows how Sherman is well on his way to losing his cushy job and the ludicrous luxary that could have been his (Sherman could have been a Lopwitz one day, we are sure.). Similarly, Sherman's poignant final visit to the bank emphasizes that such transactions –– huge cash withdrawals with respectful and eager bank staff –– will soon be a thing of the past. His financial security is as tenuous as his job. Finally, Sherman's beautiful home and family, so exquisitely furnished and maintained, is only his for another evening. Everything is coming to a head.

Particularly touching is the episode with Campbell, who (despite bearing an aggressively fashionable eighties name) is not at all responsible for the events in the book. She seems unaware of her privileges, able to be a remarkably imaginative child almost in spite of the trendiness of her upbringing. Sherman has never been able to connect with her –– even about trivial things like Santa Claus –– and now that communicating with his daughter is the most important thing in the world, his failure to cultivate their relationship shows itself to be among the greatest failures of his life. He can't even appreciate her imagination without reading into a story of a koala an allegory of his imminent arrest and imprisonment.

Of course, Sherman himself is to blame for his collapse. His reckless hubris and his failures of communication with everyone who could have potentially loved and protected him -- including his father, his wife, his daughter -- are glaringly clear. Sherman was so sure of himself -- such a "Sure Man" -- that he lost all sense of his vulnerability. This reflects his former overbearing personality, of course, but it also seems endemic to the 1980s. John McCoy, though hardly perfect, is a much steadier, much more modest and sensible man. Sherman rose in the eighties -- the "Me" decade -- and he will fall as he rose, alone.

It's almost unnecessary to continue pointing out the Dickensian name games, but John McCoy's firm is full of them: Dunning – to "dun" someone out of money; Sponget – to "sponge" money off someone; and Leach – to "leech." In addition, the secretary that John shares with the other older partners is called Miss Needleman – in that she needles the old men she works for, or needles other men on the telephone.

Summary and Analysis of Chapter 22 - "Styrofoam Peanuts" and Chapter 23 - "Inside the Cavity"

Summary

Sherman can't sleep. He's overwhelmed with fears about his coming incarceration, despite Killian's reassurances. He watches his daughter sleep and wonders at her innocence even as he's obsessed with his own guilt, then he crawls back into bed -- alone, Judy is sleeping elsewhere -- and tries to get some rest. He goes through the events of the following day in his head: he'll be picked up by the detectives at 7:30 AM, taken to Central Booking and put in a holding pen. Then he will post the agreed-upon $10,000 bond and walk free.

In the morning at breakfast Judy and Sherman cannot speak to each other. Finally, when it is time to go, Judy walks Sherman to the door and tells him, "Be brave -- remember who you are." She tries to be encouraging, but she just looks tired.

Downstairs, Sherman is handcuffed and Killian, Sherman, and the detectives get into Detective Martin's car. Detective Martin's child has left Styrofoam peanuts all over the back seat and they cover Sherman's clothing. The policemen tell Killian that DA Weiss wouldn't allow Bernie Fitzgibbon to honor his "contract," and that the media will be there to photograph Sherman as he is booked. Killian blows up because he went through trouble to secure Sherman's cooperation only to have the "contract" violated.

It has begun to rain, and outside the door that leads to Central Booking is a long line of criminals waiting to be processed. The press has arrived in force; they mob Sherman and Killian, requesting comments. Killian angrily tells the mob that this is a "circus arrest" and tries to get Sherman to the head of the line. It's impossible, as DA Weiss has insisted that Sherman get no special treatment. Sherman recognizes Peter Fallow's name from the accusatory pieces in *The City Light*. Wet, and covered with Styrofoam peanuts, Sherman looks less like Park Avenue than Bruckner Boulevard in the press photos. This later angers DA Weiss, who would have preferred pictures of a slick-looking rich white man rather than a bedraggled sad sack.

Finally, Sherman is booked, photographed, and fingerprinted. The arresting officers remove his belt and shoelaces, which causes him to lose his shoes. Sherman has to go through the metal detector repeatedly because he has so many silver fillings that it goes off every time. Detective Martin asks the booking officer if Sherman could sit at a desk rather than in the holding pen, but DA Weiss has left word that there is to be no special treatment. Sherman briefly feels a wave of gratitude to Detective Martin, but this quickly passes into fear of what's to come in the holding pen.

In the holding cell, the prisoners taunt Sherman. A drunken man vomits and is hosed down. The other prisoners question Sherman about his charges, and Sherman fabricates charges to make himself look tough. Just as a man is threatening to steal his jacket, Sherman is called upstairs.

In front of the judge at the arraignment, Larry Kramer, acting under orders from DA Weiss, tries get bail raised to $250,000. Kramer cites the community pressure and media interest in the case as his reasons, but Judge Kovitzky reminds him that public opinion doesn't drive court decisions. The bail is set at $10,000, as previously agreed upon, and Sherman is freed. Despairing, Sherman contemplates the double–barrelled shotgun he has at home, and wonders if it will fit in his mouth.

In Chapter 23, Kramer meets with DA Weiss, who praises his courtroom performance and refers to the artist's sketch of Kramer that was shown on the news. Kramer recalls the beautiful Italian court artist and wonders at the powerful sexual effect Italian women have on him. DA Weiss approves of the media coverage, especially Peter Fallow's lurid piece in *The City Light*. The press lambasts Sherman and speculates on the "foxy brunette" (Maria) who was in the car with him. Kramer leaves the meeting on good terms with Weiss and personally happy that a W.A.S.P. like Sherman is now getting a taste of the real world.

Sherman, understandably, is miserable. His life seems to have collapsed around him and he recalls the findings of a Spanish brain physiologist, Jose M. R. Delgado, who argues that the mind is much how the Amazonian Bororo Indians have asserted that it is; an open cavity connected to every other human brain. Sherman feels that the world –– the particularly ugly world of the justice system and the press –– is rooting around in the open cavity of his mind.

The press tries to contact Sherman incessantly and Sherman feels friendless aside from his father and Killian. Rawlie Thorpe, an old school chum, offers support, but Sherman is not comforted. Sherman's attempt to resume business–as–usual goes awry when the press hounds him at Campbell's bus stop. Enraged, Sherman pushes a reported; the reported immediately accuses him of assault and Campbell begins crying.

Fallow at *The City Light* gets a hold of a picture of Sherman "assaulting" the reporter and decides to publish it. We learn that Fallow has done well for himself with this story –– he has received a raise and is in his boss' good graces. Fallow also decides to give Vogel Reverend Bacon's private telephone number. He owes Vogel a favor after the story.

Analysis

Sherman is almost totally alone –– and he knows it. He sleeps alone on the night before his arrest, he stands alone (aside from his lawyer) in the line to Central Booking, and he waits alone in the holding pen. He himself, the Master of the

Universe who thought of himself so highly, has disappeared into a media metaphor for an evil white snob. No matter how foolish and arrogant Sherman has behaved, it's hard not to feel as though he is a victim of circumstances beyond his control. This is precisely what Wolfe would like us to feel -- that though Sherman is flawed, those flaws are endemic to greater social forces, and he is after all redeemable.

Judy, on the other hand, might be another story. Her only appearance in these chapters, when she tells Sherman to "Be brave" and "remember who [he is]," strikes the reader as hopelessly out–of–touch. Perhaps Judy feels that Sherman's only chance now is to adopt the arrogant attitude that took him so far in bond trading, but the reader may well feel that Judy has yet to acknowledge the extent of Sherman's fall from grace. She feels perhaps that he still has social leverage, when in fact his past "social leverage" seems to be working against him. Once again, Wolfe leaves Judy a mystery. Whereas we are granted clear access to Sherman's every anxiety, his every complexity, we are left to interpret Judy vaguely as elitist and clueless. If such is the case, it's Wolfe's failing, not Judy's.

From the novel's beginning, it has been apparent that characters act largely in accordance with racial or ethnic interests. The Jewish District Attorney Weiss seems no different. His refusal to honor Killian's and Fitzgibbon's "contract" is an example of how the media–crazy DA handles things differently than the Irish who used to run the city's legal system. The Irish "Donkey Loyalty" that protected W.A.S.P.s in the past seems to have lapsed. As Jews and Italians supplant the Irish on the police force, such old–fashioned codes of honor no longer apply -- what matters instead is media image, as captured in Weiss and Kramer. Wolfe's 1980s New York is, to a great degree, a Jewish New York (even a self–loathing Jewish New York), with a Jewish mayor a Jewish man running Pierce &Pierce and a Jewish DA. Needless to say, these are not flattering portraits, and Wolfe perhaps covers himself from charges of anti–Semitism (though the reader will judge for him or herself as to the effectiveness of his cover) with a sparkling example of a Jewish judge, Judge Kovitzky.

Meanwhile, Wolfe offers a harrowing portrait of the dehumanizing nature of the Bronx Central Booking office -- and if that's bad, imagine how horrible the prisons must be! Sherman is certainly receiving a view of things from the other side. To quote a prisoner's gratuitous reminder, "This ain't Park Avenue." Which is another way of saying, "We're not in Kansas anymore."

Summary and Analysis of Chapter 24 - "The Informants" and Chapter 25 - "We the Jury"

Summary

Sherman is irate about the circumstances of his arrest. He feels betrayed by Killian, and persecuted by the system, so he storms Killian's office in order to fire the lawyer. After an uncomfortable wait, Sherman lights into Killian, but Killian counters that he was betrayed by the DA's office. He apologizes and implies that the treatment would never have occurred if an Irishman had been DA. Killian talks too fast and too much to allow Sherman to fire him.

The lawyer calls into his office a private investigator, Quigley, who has tracked down Roland Auburn's mug shot. Sherman identifies Roland as the second man at the scene of the accident. Killian explains that Roland's criminal history make it likely that he struck a bargain to testify, which weakens the DA's case. Quigley has also tracked down Maria, who has fled with the young artist Filippo Chirazzi to Italy. Sherman gallantly insists that Maria is neither evading the court nor seeing Chirazzi. Having provided this news, Killian demands a huge retainer fee of $75,000. Sherman naively agrees.

Downtown, Lawrence Kramer and Shelly Thomas dine together at a trendy cajun restaurant. Though the food is awful, they both pretend to enjoy themselves because of the place's trendiness (and exorbitant expense). Larry agonizes over where to take Shelly so that they can be alone together. He continues to put himself and his case in the best possible light. Shelly knows that Larry is married and doesn't seem to mind. She annoys Larry, however, by observing that, as Roland is a criminal, Sherman might have been avoiding a robbery at the time of the hit–and–run. When this comment offends Larry, Shelly clams up. She allows Larry to kiss her even as she complains inwardly that New York men always talk about their careers on dates.

Peter Fallow receives another huge and undeserved break when, at the Leicester bar, a woman he had long pursued tells him the identity of the "Mystery Brunette." This informant, Caroline Heftshank, is a society friend of Maria Ruskin through Filippo Chirazzi.

In Chapter 25, Edward Fiske III continues to try to track down the $350,000 his Diocese gave Reverend Bacon. Just as before, Bacon is busy fielding phone calls about the Lamb case. Bacon tries to elude Fiske with another speech about "steam control" -- how the Diocese money is a guilty pay–off from the white establishment -- but Fiske has done his homework. He has uncovered Bacon's dummy corporation, Urban Guaranty Investments. Fiske asks Bacon to pay the Diocese back from Urban Guaranty Investments' ample funds. Bacon counters that it's illegal to "mix funds," and says that the Diocese's money has been put to good use. The Reverend's bodyguard (the tall man with the gold earring) politely escorts the "befuddled" Fiske to the door.

Meanwhile, Bacon's people have been busy. A group of angry protesters have besieged the McCoys' Park Avenue apartment. McCoy has hired, on Killian's recommendation, four body guards –– two for the Park Avenue apartment, and two for his parents' townhouse, where Judy and Campbell are staying. While Sherman chafes under death threats and calls from the media, the rapacious and impolite real estate broker whom he met at the Bavardages' cocktail party, Sally Rawthrote, calls to offer her services in selling his apartment. McCoy, enraged, tells her off and slams down the phone. The outburst raises his spirits, slightly.

Sherman also learns that Al Vogel is representing Henry Lamb in a civil suit against him. To top all, Pollard Browning, president of the apartment co–op, asks him to leave because of the ongoing protest. Sherman lets Pollard have it too, practically throwing him out of the apartment.

Analysis

After thirty–eight years of privilege and wealth, the misfortunes keep piling up for Sherman. Having received a taste of victimization (and Wolfe is careful to show how unjustified the extent of Sherman's punishment has become), Sherman is quick to feel that he doesn't deserve any of this trouble. He doesn't yet see his own flaws –– how childish his view of "us" and "them" is, and how inadaquate. Sherman has yet to take responsibility for the mess he is in, which followed quite clearly from his own racism, denial, old–fashioned chivalry, and legal stupidity.

That's not to say that he's not growing at all. The affair has made the inanity of his Park Avenue lifestyle clearer and clearer, and this realization is leading Sherman to act out of indignation rather than despair. The outbursts Sherman has to Sally Rawthrote and Pollard Browning, both Park Avenue establishment types, show that he is nearing the end of his patience. He realizes now that he has never had any real friends in his Park Avenue world, and he is disgusted that everyone has turned on him in his hour of need. Killian jokes that Sherman is "turning Irish," because he has some fight in him now. Once a suicidal W.A.S.P., Sherman seems to realize –– or to be on the verge of realizing –– that a little Irish isn't a bad thing. If he's going to get out of this, he'll have to get angry and fight. Despite this newfound fire, however, the question of whether Sherman will move beyond indignation and disgust with Park Avenue, and toward a greater understanding of others, remains open.

Meanwhile, Killian is as smooth as ever –– perhaps he's named after the lager? He staves off McCoy's obvious attempts to broach the subject of firing him, and even manages to hit up Sherman for a bundle while Sherman still has money to give. Additionally, the private investigator Quigley seems to have made some real progress in the case, having found out Maria's whereabouts and Roland's criminal history.

It's worth noting that although McCoy has been crucified by the media, his case is not really all that bleak. Manslaughter at worst, yes, but if he can either undermine Roland's credibility as a witness (which, given his plea–bargain and his criminal history, isn't that mighty a task) *or* establish that Maria was the driver (which, after all, she was), Sherman's off the hook. The case has been inflated into an opened–and–closed affair by the media, which could ultimately work against the prosecution as much as the defense.

Case in point: Larry Kramer. Even Shelly can see that Larry's case is wobbly, but Larry is so intoxicated by his newfound power and prestige that he has no realistic sense of how to win the case. He feels that everything will go his way because he's the good guy on the T.V. That's the reason Shelly like him, he thinks, and the reason he can do no wrong in prosecuting the case, which is practically won already. We'll see about that.

Summary and Analysis of Chapter 26 - "Death New York Style" and Chapter 27 - "Hero of the Hive"

Summary

In Sir Gerald Steiner's office at *The City Light*, Peter Fallow and his colleagues discuss the lucky tip that Fallow received about Maria Ruskin. So they know who the Mysterious Brunette is, now what to do about it? Sir Gerald decides to send Fallow to do a profile on Maria's husband, the charter plane magnate Arthur Ruskin. Peter is to disguise his intention of getting information on Maria by interviewing her husband on his career and lavish lifestyle.

Arthur Ruskin, not usually a media hound, is nevertheless willing to have a meeting with Peter. Arthur suggests that they have dinner at La Boue d'Argent (which translated means either "mud money" or "silver mud"). When they arrive, the staff genuflects to Mr. Ruskin; another eminent guest is also arriving, Madame Tacaya, the wife of an Indonesian dictator.

Ruskin, who is 71 and disallowed alcohol by doctor's orders, nonetheless orders a sidecar with VSOP Cognac. He tells of how he rose in fortune, lost it all, and then rose even higher than before with his charter airplane business. Arthur Ruskin is a Jewish man, jokes about he and his fellow "Yids." He notes ironically that he accrued his obscene fortune by ferrying Muslims to the holy city of Mecca. Arthur is in rare (though offensive) form, and he stuffs himself with food and wine.

Suddenly, Arthur has a fit and falls to the floor. Peter helplessly calls for assistance, but the waitstaff is too busy preparing for Madame Tacaya's entrance to heed him. Paramedics arrive and take the body away. The head waiter, without missing a beat, presents Peter with the bill and is about to force Peter to pay despite his protestations when Madame Tacaya arrives, allowing Peter to escape. He runs a piece in *The City Light* the next day describing the restaurant's disregard for Mr. Ruskin, entitled, "Death New York Style."

In Chapter 27, Sherman is concerned again that he is "hemorrhaging money," as his lawyers and bodyguards cost a fortune and he has no income. Things aren't all bad, however, as a reporter named Flannagan on *The Daily News* has written an article countering the claims about the Lamb case in *The City Light*. Judy agrees to attend a party with Sherman at the di Ducci's to "keep up appearances."

At "the hive," Sherman's sobriquet for such society events, the buzzing is about him. Mrs. di Ducci, a particularly beautiful society matron, makes Judy and Sherman feel very welcome, and Sherman relishes the attention. He tells harrowing exaggerations about his time in the holding pen, and he enjoys the reputation that he has in the papers as a financial "boy wonder." The society folks humor him as a sort of curiosity, and Judy, though she stands by him at the party, tells Sherman once they leave that he's too easily pleased.

Meanwhile, the Episcopal Bishop of New York, an African–American man, discusses the fate of a small church building with the Mayor of New York. There has been some controversy over whether or not it's a landmark, but the Bishop assures the Mayor that it is not an important building, and it's in the best interests of the Diocese that it be sold. The Mayor, wanting to curry favor with black voters but as yet unwilling to call for fierce prosecution of the McCoy case, is happy to oblige, as long as the Bishop serves on a "special blue–ribbon commission on crime" in return. The Bishop cannot possibly do so, according to the rules of his Diocese, and so he politely refuses and leaves. The Mayor, in revenge, calls the Landmark Commission and tells them to immediately grant landmark status to the church building in question.

Analysis

The chapter involving the life–story and the dramatic death of Arthur Ruskin is perhaps the most blackly humorous of the novel. Arthur is drawn in vivid detail. We have learned from Maria that Arthur is verbally abusive, but at dinner he is a charming and interesting character from a pre–politically correct era. He seems very much in love with the material things of life, which adds obvious irony to the colossally unkind wait staff at La Boue d'Argent. Like most things in the novel, their cruelty is a cartoon designed to capture the callousness of capitalism in the 1980s. Arthur exists for them only as a credit card. When he's dead, they have no interest in him any longer. So much for the life Arthur loves.

McCoy &McCoy Associates, as Sherman calls his alliance with Judy to save their social reputation, is hard at work. On one level this attempt to resume life as normal, and to save whatever vestiges of dignity and status that they can, represents Sherman McCoy's newfound resolve to fight. However, one might ask how realistic the attempt is. Sherman's motive is clear, but what about Judy's? Is Judy still hurt that Sherman pursued Maria and lied to her about it? Is she intent on preserving their home? Does she secretly love Sherman? We have no idea, because, as thoughout the novel, Wolfe leaves the inner–lives of his female characters a mystery. Her willingness to "stand by her man" in public is never explained.

We know that the novel is rounding to a close because characters who have been absent for hundreds of pages –– Fiske, for example –– have begun to pop up again. The Mayor is one of these. His portrait in Chapter 27 is no more flattering than our first view of him at the riot. He breathes politics, and has no honest regard for the welfare of the city, only for the security of his office. The meeting with the Bishop is a chilling glimpse at tit–for–tat City politics. The Bishop, as a black man, would have lent a modicum of credibility to his proposed crime commission. Instead, because he can't get any support from a black man, the Mayor feels that he is forced to malign McCoy to regain his credibility with non–white voters.

The offensively humorous "plaques for blacks" discussion with Sheldon, the Mayor's secretary, shows the kind of "for the media only" activities that the City uses for "steam control" –– i.e. to throw the civil rights activists an occasional bone. The Mayor sees his reputation with African–Americans as dependant upon an occassional plaque and photo op. Neither Reverend Bacon nor the Mayor seems to think that real social reform or racial healing is at all possible. Indeed, both of them seem invested in maintaining a status quo of racial divide; their power depends on it. Steam control indeed.

Summary and Analysis of Chapter 28 - "Off to a Better Place" and Chapter 29 - "The Rendezvous"

Summary

Killian and Quigley encourage Sherman to talk to Maria while wearing a wire in order to establish that she was driving the car at the time of the accident. Sherman knows that he will be able to see her at her husband's funeral, and he's not sure that he's ever going to get to talk to her again. It takes some doing, but Killian and Quigley convince Sherman to try the wire idea.

Arthur's funeral is a lavish affair at the best funeral parlor, Harold A. Burns's on Madison Avenue. A significant number of important socialites are present. Maria, beautifully dressed in an expensive black suit, plays the demurely grieving widow. Peter Fallow lurks about noting who has entered so as to write–up the event in *The City Light.* He peeks in the guest book for names (noting some of the vapid social animals Sherman has encountered at the Bavardages' and di Duccis', such as Baron Hochswald, Nunnally Voyd, and Bobby Shaflett).

Sherman approaches Maria while they are in earshot of Peter Fallow. Fallow overhears him say to her, "But you're my only witness." Maria says nothing of value for Sherman's tape, but Fallow has (once again) struck gold. He hears Maria pronounce Sherman's name "Shuhmun," which coincides with Roland Auburn's memory. Fallow decides to crucify Sherman and Maria both.

Once Sherman leaves, Fallow approaches Maria and explains that he was with her husband when he died. He lies and says that he tried to help Arthur by providing CPR. At first she is demure and grateful, but when he changes the subject to Sherman and the accident, she strongly rebuffs him.

In Chapter 29, Kramer, Bernie Fitzgibbon, Detective Martin, and Detective Goldberg all meet in Abe Weiss's office. Their case has hit a snag. Two crack dealers have come forward willing to talk about Roland Auburn in exchange for lighter sentencing. They say that they have information about the night of the Lamb ordeal.

These witnesses state that Roland Auburn had been teasing Henry Lamb at the Texas Fried Chicken stand because of Henry's law–abiding, churchgoing ways. Roland egged Henry into watching him "take off" a car (meaning "rob the occupants and strip the car of valuables"). He brought Henry to an expressway on–ramp and blocked the ramp with a tire. Henry did not help him, though he was present. The young man say that the Mercedes came along and a confrontation took place between the two young men and Sherman and Maria; Henry was sideswiped by the Mercedes as it sped off.

DA Weiss is furious. This new take on the event compromises Roland's testimony, which is Kramer's main line of evidence. Bernie Fitzgibbon notes that the new story matches the story that Sherman told to the *Daily News*. It also explains certain holes in Roland's account, such as why Henry didn't tell anyone at the hospital that he was hit by a car. They do wonder why Roland would want someone as inexperienced and "lame" as Henry along on a robbery attempt.

Kramer, who is by now professionally committed to the case, attempts to defend Roland. A colleague interrupts with an article from *The City Light* that fingers Maria as the Mysterious Brunette. Weiss springs into action, informing the media, and sends Kramer, Martin, and Goldberg to interview Maria and threaten her with the "he hit, she ran" scenario. He plans to bring felony charges against her unless she testifies against McCoy.

Kramer with the media in tow (thanks to Weiss), confronts Maria, who has already secured two attorneys, and spooks her with the felony threat. Her luxuriant apartment -- even more impressive than the McCoys' -- makes for ideal news coverage, and Larry gets a sick thrill out of asserting his power over her.

Meanwhile Tommy Killian and Sherman discuss the *City Lights* article. Apparently Maria has contacted Killian, asking to meet Sherman "you know where" at 4:30. Sherman prepares to wear a wire to their interview.

Sherman arrives at the hideaway apartment, seeing it with new, jaundiced eyes. They had felt the place to be a deliciously "bohemian" retreat; in fact, it's just dingy. He meets Maria, who insists that she knew nothing about Sherman's legal trouble when she went to Italy, but rather intended to escape Arthur's "verbal abuse." This is a lie, which Sherman knows because he showed her the first *City Light* article himself. She dodges, however, and Sherman tries to steer the conversation to the accident, hoping to get her to admit to driving the car on tape.

Maria moves to hug him, and Sherman awkwardly shifts so that she doesn't feel the hidden tape recorder. She tells Sherman about Kramer's threat, saying that she must corroborate the DA's case to avoid felony charges. Sherman continues to fish for a confession, and Maria notices his awkwardness. She embraces him again and feels the tape recorder. Sherman flees the apartment, feeling like a failure and a cheat, with her insults ringing in his ears.

Analysis

The funeral of Arthur Ruskin reprises the parties at the Bavardages' and the di Ducci's. Many of the same people are there, and the atmosphere of wealthy self–congratulation is the same. Wolfe thus satires the New York elite in a most macabre manner. There is no relief from social convention or pretentiousness, not even in death. Once again, even Fallow finds the remorseless superficiality of these W.A.S.P. monsters unbearable. Even their eulogies smack of insincerity.

Slowly but surely, Sherman is coming to see such nonsense clearly. He has even lost his rose–tinted glasses with Maria, whose standoffish behavior at the funeral betrays a ferocious selfishness. Indeed, Maria is depicted as little more than a Jezebel -- a two–timing flirt who would happily leave Sherman to rot in jail if she weren't implicated in the mess by Fallow. Her attempts to use seductive wiles to discover his strategy are no better than Sherman's recourse to a wire. Indeed, Sherman's approach is more dignified in the eyes of the reader, simply because he's in pursuit of the truth -- she *was* driving the car, after all -- while she is willing to lie to save her neck. If the shoe were on the other foot -- if Sherman had been driving and she were called to account for it -- you can bet that noble, gallant Sherman would have rushed to her defense. More fool he, perhaps.

Maria's seductive duplicity, like so many elements in this novel, follows from age–old stereotypes. She is the shallow, forked–tongue, painted city woman from time out of mind -- and Wolfe gives her no character whatever aside from this stereotype. Indeed, one of the concerns of his book seems to be a reexamination of the old gender stereotypes, and not a generous one. If women have *always* been wily, and men has *always* suffered for it, perhaps (Wolfe suggests) it's time for men to give up the noble approach and wear a wire to save their skins. In a world where everyone else is strategic, the honest perish quick. Perhaps one can thus forgive Wolfe his incessant stereotyping (and his inability to write convincing women characters) by arguing that *everyone* in the book is a lying bounder. But Wolfe still lends redeemable traits to his men, especially to Sherman, that he denies his women. If there is one major stumbling block for the reader of *The Bonfire of the Vanities*, it's Wolfe's apparent disinterest in characters who aren't white men.

The emergence of (not exactly credible, but no less so than Roland) witnesses that corroborate McCoy's story is crucial. For one thing, it guarantees the futility of Kramer's quest for The Great White Defendant, though he's not giving up yet. It also tweaks the events of the night in question one more time. Apparently the black men *were* going to rob the white folks in the Bronx; apparently the white folks were justified in speeding away so fearfully.

But even as Wolfe provides this apparent endorsement of racial prejudice, he complicates matters with the development of Henry's character. Henry is a good kid, whose mother was evidently working with him on his future, who was sucked into a stupid and senseless robbery without his consent. Following the accident, Henry probably knew that, even if he told the truth, he'd somehow be blamed -- as young African–American men often are -- for what Roland attempted, and so he kept quiet about the collision and thus failed to receive treatment for his head injury. Responsibility for Henry's death is complicated; it implicates the culture of fear and mistrust toward black men just as clearly as it implicates the criminal culture of Roland. He is indeed a Lamb sacrificed to all of society.

Summary and Analysis of Chapter 30 - "An Able Pupil"; Chapter 31 – "Into the Solar Plexus" and Epilogue – "Financier Is Arraigned"

Summary

At the courthouse, the grand jury is assembled for the McCoy indictment. Roland Auburn is brought forward to give evidence. Tommy Killian, Sherman's lawyer, cannot be there, as this is an indictment and not a hearing or a trial, and Larry Kramer takes advantage of this to make Roland Auburn look as presentable as possible. Larry has taught Roland to walk, at least temporarily, without the "Pimp Roll" which so clearly says "Street Hood" to a jury. Instead, Roland wears "preppy" clothes. Roland tells the story we know already, changing the location and details of the event to make it seem that he and Henry Lamb were innocent victims of Sherman's callousness and carelessness. He is sure to note that he heard the woman refer to "Shuhmun."

Maria Ruskin, dressed to the nines, is called to the stand. She plays the young, beautiful, grieving widow and manages to look both trustworthy and glamorous. She corroborates the details of Roland's testimony, agreeing that the incident occurred on Bruckner Boulevard and telling the jury that Sherman was driving when Henry was hit. She also says that Sherman refused to tell the police. Larry makes Maria say "Shuhmun" many times. The grand jury indicts Sherman.

The City Light runs an article about the rent–controlled "hideaway" apartment that Maria illegally sublet from her friend, Germaine Boll. Sherman and his legal team discuss Maria, and Sherman (incredibly) clings to his feeling that she has "walked a straight line" in the affair. Quigley and Killian, on the other hand, see Maria as little better than a high–class hooker. The news article has a provocative photo of Maria, and says that she lured McCoy, and possibly others, into her "love nest." Judy will undoubtedly see the article, and McCoy frets that he has lied to Judy; now she is certain never to forgive him.

Sherman wonders how Fallow could have gotten the information about the rent–controlled nature of the illegal hideaway. Sherman never told anyone, and Maria has no reason to incriminate herself. Quigley guesses that the landlord, Mr. Winter, must be illegally monitoring the property in order to evict rent–controlled tenants in favor of higher–paying tenants, and he rushes out to test his theory. Meanwhile, Bernie Fitzgibbon calls Killian, and tells him about the indictment and the possibility of increased bail. Sherman faces possible jail time once more.

Larry Kramer also sees the article in *The City Light*. He grants that the depiction of Maria will harm her in front of a jury, but relaxes because the grand jury indictment has already occurred. The comment about a "rent–controlled love nest, $331 a month" catches his interest, and he toys with the idea of calling the landlord, Mr. Winter, for information.

That night, Sherman despairs of going back to jail. The luxury of his surroundings mock him. He calls Judy in Southampton, but receives no comfort from her. She has given up on the relationship. Sherman recalls a shared memory of when he was a young upstart in finances: he would raise his fist in the Black Power salute every morning to show that though he worked on Wall Street, he was not *of* Wall Street. Judy does not respond to such memories except to say that they are "abused."

The next day, Killian calls Sherman with good news: Quigley has managed to obtain a recording of Maria and Sherman talking together in the hideaway. Apparently Mr. Winter, attempting to glean information about his leasees, hid a microphone in each apartment. Quigley has the recording from the night after the first article in *The City Light*. This is an illegal tape obtained in an illegal way, so Killian doesn't want to get Sherman's hopes up too high, but nonetheless Maria has admitted, on tape, that she was the driver at the time of the accident. Maria can thus be proved a liar and perhaps even tried for perjury.

Sherman agrees to say that he made the recording himself in order that it might be admitted as evidence. Sherman –– once a Master of the Universe, a golden boy of Wall Street –– realizes that he has sunk to the level of a criminal, but also realizes that he has to play the game that way. He is not "above" anything, and facing another stint in jail, he decides to save his own neck by any means necessary.

In Chapter 31, Sherman's bail hearing falls on a beautiful day, which Sherman takes as grimly ironic given that he might return to jail. The usual demonstrators wait for him at the court, with Peter Fallow hollering for a statement and Reverend Bacon's bodyguard amid the crowd as well. In the courtroom, Judge Myron Kovitsky presides over an unruly courtroom full of Bacon's agitators. Kovitsky, a fair and just judge, quiets the demonstrators by threatening them with contempt of court.

Larry Kramer asks for a one million dollar bail for Sherman, citing "community pressure." Killian then approaches the bench and tells Kovitsky and Kramer that he has a tape–recorded conversation between Maria and Sherman that disproves her grand jury testimony. Kramer panics and tries to block the evidence, but Kovitsky insists upon hearing the tapes in his chambers. Quigley has edited the tapes in order to make them seem legal. In them, Maria insults Kramer and insinuates that he coached her testimony. She also states that she was driving the Mercedes when she hit Henry Lamb.

Though he could follow through on the question of whether Kramer suborned purjury from Maria, Kovitsky concentrates instead on the tainted nature of the grand jury testimony. Kramer desperately attempts to defend the grand jury indictment. When Kovitsky won't budge, Kramer suggests that he will buckle before the angry mob outside. Kovitsky quietly says that he will face them down. He asserts the abstract priciples of law and justice in an angry tirade.

Kovitsky returns to the courtroom and dismisses the indictment of Sherman. However, the DA's office has the option, with further evidence, to prosecute the case in the future. The mob grows violent and Kovitsky realizes that he should have explained to the tainted nature of the grand jury evidence. A full–fledged riot breaks out. In the struggle, Sherman punches the tall, black gold–earringed bodyguard in the solar plexus. Sherman, the judge, and the lawyers escape through the back and pack into an elevator together.

Once on the ground floor, in a display of moral bravura, the judge attempts to explain himself and end the violence. However, Reverend Bacon has whipped the crowd into a frenzy. A crazed man runs violently at the judge and Sherman shoves the man away. Realizing the futility of their cause, they flee.

The Epilogue takes the form of a story in *The New York Times* by a reporter who was not involved in the McCoy case. It is dated one year after the bail hearing.

Sherman McCoy's legal woes contine and he continues to be harrassed by Reverend Bacon's political machine. As he says, "I have nothing to do with Wall Street and Park Avenue. I'm a professional defendant." Arraigned for manslaughter and sprting injuries that he apparently received behind bars, McCoy pleads "absolutely innocent." He represents himself in the arraignment, as he can no longer afford Killian's services. (Killian, however, still comments on McCoy's behalf, saying that the real criminals in the case are Bacon, Weiss and Fallow.)

Sherman's financial woes have also come to a head. He is reduced to living in a small apartment, and his remaining money is frozen as a result of civil actions brought by Vogel. A Bronx jury awarded Henry Lamb $12 million in damages, a decision that Sherman is appealing.

We learn that McCoy had attempted to give his apartment and remaining assets to his ex–wife (yes, Judy has divorced him) and daughter. Judy and Campbell have moved back to Wisconsin, but Judy appeared in the courtroom at the arraignment. Sherman gave her the Black Power salute, but has since refused to speak to reporters about it.

Because Kovitsky threw out the previous indictment, the Bronx Democratic organization refused to re–nominate him and he was defeated. When Sherman was re–indicted by a different grand jury in February, the trial resulted in a hung jury.

Meanwhile, Maria has married the artist Filippo Chirazzi. Also, we learn that Larry Kramer has been removed from the case after trying to secure Maria's rent–controlled hideaway for his affair with Shelly Thomas. Herbert 92X, the man Kramer was prosecuting when he met Shelly, has obtained a reversal of his first–degree manslaughter conviction on the grounds of prosecutorial misconduct.

Fallow, we learn, has won a Pulitzer Prize for his coverage of the McCoy case. At the book's end, he sails the Aegean Sea with his new bride, Lady Evelyn, Sir Gerald Steiner's daughter.

Analysis

Wolfe sets up the farcical grand jury indictment almost as a collection of "oppressed groups fighting back" against Sherman, the poster boy for the W.A.S.P. ruling class, with Roland representing African–Americans, Maria representing women, Larry representing Jews and the whole lot representing the lower classes (even Maria had humble origins in South Carolina). The fact that this band of the "oppressed" are using the criminal justice system to pursue their grievances, and the fact that every one of them is guilty of purjury, undermines the whole notion of "striking back" against "the man." Some might consider Wolfe's entire purpose satirical –– after all, aside from Judge Kovitsky, it's nearly impossible to find a principled adult in the story, and we don't know Kovitsky too well.

However, the care with which he sets up the opposition of a flawed but redeemable W.A.S.P. with a pack of rampant power–hungry perjurors suggests a broader message. Wolfe seems to condemn the idea that one can punish an individual for the crimes of his race. Though the white establishment may be guilty of horrible crimes, Sherman McCoy, Wolfe suggests, is innocent, and only lies and travesties can bring him down.

As this analysis has noted repeatedly, Wolfe has a great deal of sympathy for Sherman McCoy, the embattled white man. He ultimately justifies his racist reaction to the Lamb incident by establishing that Roland intended to rob him; he presents his actions toward Maria as noble and self–sacrificing even to the point of absurdity; he submits Sherman to incredibly unjust (and unrealistic, even for the culture wars of the eighties) persecution by Fallow's pen and Bacon's mob. In short, it's impossible to feel that Sherman McCoy deserves the heap of trouble he gets, no matter how predisposed one is to despise him.

Yet surely McCoy deserves *some* trouble! After all, he did cover up a hit–and–run, he has committed and covered–up adultery, he has repeatedly demonstrated a knee–jerk aversion to African–Americans, and he has coasted to millions without special insight into the workings of the world, simply on the basis of his pedigree. Throughout the novel, one waits for the moment when McCoy's understanding of society expands, when he takes the world in from a perspective other than his own. Alas, it never comes. The most Sherman can manage is a cynical rejection of superficial Park Avenue affectations. Is this Sherman's great triumph? To see how shallow rich New Yorkers can be? Because such a conclusion will surprise few. Yet

Wolfe appears to endorse this conclusion in the epilogue, when he has Sherman salute his wife with a black power fist -- as though he is justified now, after a year of legal woes, in identifying with the permanent urban underclass in the Bronx. This is character progress? It seems, rather, like the substitution of one self–indulgent Master of the Universe fantasy for another.

But then one wrongs Wolfe, perhaps, by taking his apparent messages too seriously -- and heck, perhaps Wolfe expects us to see so clearly through McCoy's affected "absolute innocen[ce]." *The Bonfire of the Vanities* is a work of satire, after all, filled with curmudgeonly asides (notice how often Wolfe decries sneakers as evidence of social decay) and cartoonish overstatement. Perhaps, with this in mind, Wolfe wishes to present in his novel the eighties as he sees them, through a journalist's jaundiced eye. The city, the era seem like a drawn–out cynical morality play, with no side deserving of applause but each protesting its virtue with loudspeakers and photo ops. Its the era of demagogues from both camps -- a DA Weiss for every Reverend Bacon -- who depend on perpetuating the status quo, on feeding racism where it exists and fanning it up where it doesn't. The more racism there is, the more power Bacon has, this seems clear. And the less justice there is, the more power Weiss has. Two perfect paradoxes, and we're caught in the middle. What can we do but laugh?

Such a bitter, comic view finds much to back it up in the absurd epilogue. It appears that Sherman's mire of legal troubles, criminal and civil, will never be resolved. Maria, of course, gets off scot–free and marries Filippo. Kovitsky, the spokesperson for morality in the novel, loses his office because of the McCoy case. Al Vogel, the man who orchestrated the public anger over this case in the first place, wins a massive judgment against Sherman and the hospital, and no doubt collects his fee. Larry Kramer, devolved to a caricature of lust and stupidity, is caught foolishly trying to rent the "hideaway" for his affair with Shelly Thomas. Killian, unable to represent Sherman anymore because he's already taken all of his available assets, is in legal trouble of his own. And Fallow, who is, possibly after Al Vogel, the person who caused the most damage of all, wins the highest honor in journalism and marries a rich aristocrat. *C'est la vie.*

Suggested Essay Questions

1. Many of the names of characters in Bonfire of the Vanities are clearly allegorical. Henry Lamb, the sacrificial victim of the Great White Defendant, is the most obvious example. Discuss some other character names and what these names reveal. What is Wolfe trying to say with them. Some good examples are Reverend Bacon, Peter Fallow, and Thomas Killian, but any of the characters can be analyzed.
2. What is the importance in Kramer's and other characters' minds of "Irish Masculinity," as represented by Detective Martin, Bernie Fitzgibbon, and Thomas Killian? Do you agree that everyone involved in criminal justice, including Jewish people and other ethnicities, became "Irish" by association? What does Wolfe mean by "Irish Masculinity," exactly? Is it a positive or negative trait in the criminal justice system? How much of it is posturing and how much is real?
3. Discuss the depiction of women in this novel. The main characters are all men, with women as wives or girlfriends or, occasionally, associates to the men. Do you consider any of Wolfe's female characters sympathetic? What in the depiction of Judy McCoy, for example, makes her a sympathetic character, and what are her faults? Do you see any of the female characters as "round" or "whole" characters? For that matter, is there a difference in Wolfe's treatment of men and women?
4. The original bonfires of the vanities occurred in Renaissance Europe, particularly Italy, when "sinful" objects such as fine clothing, immoral books and paintings, and even mirrors were burned publicly by Catholic conservatives. Most famously, these bonfires were conducted by the reactionary priest Savonarola in the 15th century. How does this phrase, used as the title for Wolfe's book, relate to the story? What was the metaphorical "bonfire" of what 20th century "vanities"? What do you consider were the "vanities" in Sherman McCoy's life, for example?
5. A number of commentaries claim that Reverend Bacon is based on the real life Reverend Al Sharpton. Do you think that there is any similarity between the character and the man? Is the comparison insulting? What do you think of Fiske and Fallow's idea that Bacon may be a kind of guerilla society leader? Are the beyond–and–above the law practices of Reverend Bacon, in your view, warranted in a racist society, or merely the actions of a criminal? Use examples from the text of how the Reverend Bacon's actions can be seen as either criminal or justified.
6. The social and ethnic snobbery of Sherman McCoy and his peers reaches a suffocating level in Bonfire of the Vanities. Sherman seems to categorize everyone in his world on ethnic and social terms. Explain how this thick fog of prejudice affects Sherman in his business and personal life.
7. Discuss one of the subplots, and explain what it adds to the novel. For example, examine The Detectives Martin and Goldberg subplot, the Fiske–Bacon subplot, the discussion between the Episcopal Bishop of New

York and the Mayor of New York, the entire description of Peter Fallow, the heckling by the prisoners of Kramer and Judge Kovitzky, or any other periphery event you wish.

8. Does the fact that Sherman has a child, Campbell, have any bearing on the novel? What is revealed about Sherman in his interactions with Campbell? How are children generally treated in Sherman's Park Avenue world? Were Sherman's actions more or less justified, regarding the accident, when viewed in light of his status as a father of a young child?
9. How does Reverend Bacon use the "fronts" of his charitable and church organizations, such as the Little Shepherd Day Care center, and the Third World Anti–Defamation league? Could a group composed of any other race or ethnicity (in Tom Wolfe's 1980s New York) have gotten away with such practices? Explain how the extortion and influence–peddling works, and how it relates to the Reverend's use of the media. How does the white power structure's guilt about African–Americans affect these illegal practices?
10. Is the complete dismantling of Sherman McCoy's life a fit punishment for his "crimes"? Explain whether you think that Sherman's actions were criminal. Does the novel cast a sinister light on Sherman, or paint him sympathetically?
11. Discuss Wolfe's writing style. Examine his linguistic tricks, like allegorically–charged names, as well as his style in general. What is Wolfe's tone throughout the novel? Does it change? On the whole, is Wolfe's novel comic or serious or both?

Controversy over the making of the film The Bonfire of the Vanities

The novel *The Bonfire of the Vanities* was made into a film, released in 1990. Brian DePalma, a director best known for *Scarface*, directed the film. The film was beset by problems from its studio, Warner Brothers, which required that certain actors be contracted to play certain parts.

Tom Hanks played Sherman McCoy, with a supporting cast that included Bruce Willis as Peter Fallow, Melanie Griffith as Maria Ruskin, Morgan Freeman as Judge Leonard White, and Kim Cattrall as Judy McCoy. The script was written by playwright Michael Cristofer.

The filming itself aroused considerable controversy. Not unlike the kind of "community pressure" cited in the novel as a driving force for the prosecution of Sherman McCoy, certain community groups that objected to the negative way in which the Bronx was depicted. Filmmakers agreed show more positive features of the Bronx: its zoo and botanical gardens, and the beauty of some of its architecture. There are also considerable differences between Wolfe's story and the film, such as Sherman's acquittal, his defense attorney, the judge's moralistic speech, and the character of Maria Ruskin. The film also lost the ambiguity of whether Sherman's car actually hit Henry Lamb or not, a point which informs most of the satirical thrust of the novel.

The convoluted process of the changes to the script and casting are chronicled in *The Devil's Candy*, a book by Julie Salamon. The movie was a flop at the box office, which was surprising because of the popularity of the novel, the A–list director and stars, and the amount of money spent on the production. The extensive changes to the script were entirely the result of Warner Brothers' desires; Wolfe, who had nothing to do with either the screenplay or the production, has been quoted as saying "I've never wanted to write any script based on something I've done."

Author of ClassicNote and Sources

Elizabeth Smith, author of ClassicNote. Completed on March 04, 2007, copyright held by GradeSaver.

Updated and revised W.C. Miller April 17, 2007. Copyright held by GradeSaver.

Wolfe, Tom. The Bonfire of the Vanities. New York: Farrar, Straus, Giroux, 1987.

Salaman, Julie. The Devil's Candy: The Bonfire of the Vanities Goes to Hollywood. Boston: Houghton Mifflin Company, 1991.

Wolfe, Tom. In Our Time. New York: Farrar, Straus, Giroux, 1961.

McKeen, William. Tom Wolfe. New York: Twayne Publishers, 1995.

Teachout, Terry, ed. Boyond the Boom: New Voices on American Life, Culture, and Politics. New York: Poseidon Press, 1990.

Scura, Dorothy M., ed.. Conversations with Tom Wolfe. Jackson, Mississippi: University Press of Mississippi, 1990.

Dictionary.com Unabridged. "Dictionary.com." Lexico Publishing Group L.L.C. 2006–01–01. 2007–03–01. <http://dictionary.reference.com/>.

Essay: The Bonfire of Veracity

by Josh M Knapp
February 27, 2005

The world that we live in is governed by a certain reality: when events take place, the fact that they happened becomes an absolute truth. Human beings, however, have the freedom to skew that truth by lying. Why, and under what conditions, would we be dishonest about things that have happened? This is one of the many questions that Tom Wolfe addresses in his novel "The Bonfire of the Vanities". Wolfe satirizes 1980s New York City using stereotypes and exaggeration. Many of Wolfe's characters are willing to disregard the truth if it serves their own selfish needs. Because these characters represent the society of that era, Wolfe is conveying the idea that the denizens of 1980s New York City are more than willing to twist the truth when it suits them. Furthermore, even individuals who originally intend to stick to the truth will be forced to stray from it as a consequence of all the other corruption. Sometimes what is considered "true" can be so far from actual fact that truth becomes almost irrelevant. Consequently, he who sets out to abide by the truth must, at times, disregard it in the name of practicality. In essence, New York has become a place where everyone must eventually, in one way or another, discount the truth.

A character who discounts the truth from the very beginning of the novel is Peter Fallow, a British reporter. When Fallow first hears about the Lamb case, he begins to construct a story around it. He includes details that he knows to be false, such as the fact that Henry Lamb was an honor student. He also declares questionable evidence to be absolutely true, and exaggerates facts. He is unsure as to whether or not the story he is printing is true, but he prints it nevertheless because he knows it will bring him fame and recognition. His own selfish needs override any concern for the truth. Wolfe uses Fallow to represent the media of the time as a whole, thereby conveying the idea that the media is an untruthful institution. The newspapers are more concerned with sales than with truth, so they take Fallow's story at face value, without bothering to check his story. This demonstrates how one person's disregard for the truth can create a snowballing problem, eventually corrupting society as a whole. The media in New York is a shining example of how dishonesty and self–interest can breed a culture of deceit.

Two other figures who put self–interest before truth are District Attorney Abe Weiss, and the Mayor. Both characters, in response to the Lamb case, only take actions that will bring them the respect of the people, regardless of whether these actions are founded in truth and justice. These two characters are representatives of the politicians of the time, who are only concerned with the election. Their actions in the Lamb case are governed by what they think the people want. For example, before the Lamb case becomes a hot topic, Weiss plans on giving it up due to lack of evidence. When the people start attacking his office for failing to take action, however, Weiss changes his position and loses his concern for the truth, because he wants to please the people and get elected. This is another example of how a corrupt society can corrupt individual people, as it does Weiss and the Mayor. In Wolfe's estimation, the public figures in 1980s New York City are acting only out of concern for their campaigns, and not based on their desire to uphold fact and morality.

Sherman McCoy's development is another example of how New Yorkers must often to stray from morality in order to survive. An innocent man, Sherman is accused of having run over a young black male, Henry Lamb. Because of the racial nature of this case, the entire city is easily convinced of Sherman's guilt. While an innocent should ordinarily be able to prove himself simply by telling the truth, the residents of New York are so egocentric and accustomed to disregarding the truth that one must play by their immoral rules even in order to prove oneself innocent. Essentially, Sherman is forced to lie in the name of the truth, telling a falsehood about a piece of evidence in order to get himself off the hook: "Sherman sat down to learn the manly art of entrapment. 'Not entrapment,' he said to himself. 'Truth'" (Wolfe, 572). Even though Sherman knows that it is wrong to lie, he assures himself that it is acceptable in the name of the greater justice. Here, Wolfe is demonstrating that even the most honest man must eventually sink to the level of the dishonest public. Even though Sherman originally intends to stick to the truth, his corruption represents the impossibility of wading through the city's sinfulness unscathed.

Does Wolfe, then, believe that it is entirely impossible for New Yorkers to maintain a concern for the truth? The only character who actually holds on to his appreciation for the truth is Judge Kovitsky. Kovitsky is originally portrayed as a powerful man, willing to stand up to criminals who are taunting him by spitting on them. In the end of the novel, he is given the task of making the final decision about Sherman's guilt. Even though he is pressured by the public both in and out of the courtroom, Kovitsky stands by his beliefs and the tenets of the law. He even attacks Larry Kramer, the prosecutor:

What makes you think you can come before the bench waving a banner of community pressure? The law is not a creature of the few or of the many....Those that come into courtrooms waving banners lose their arms! (Wolfe, 648)

Kovitsky is swayed by Sherman's case and believes that he is telling the truth, so he throws out the indictment. Even though doing this is in his best interests, he places the truth before his own needs. After he makes his judgment, the courtroom is stormed by angry people, and he and Sherman are almost killed. Here, Wolfe is expressing the belief that it takes more than a single honest man to overcome the sinfulness of New York City, and that to perpetuate the ideal of truthfulness leaves one vulnerable to attack.

In "The Bonfire of the Vanities", Wolfe creates an image of a New York City populated by individuals who unfailingly put themselves before their morals. Even those who want to be honest are forced to conform to the dishonesty of the culture.

In this society, it's not enough to want to be honest; one must have backbone and tenacity, like Kovistky. Perhaps this is why the '80s were dubbed "The Me Decade"; everyone put themselves before anything else. In the end, we must ask: does Wolfe think that there is hope for New York? Maybe, if people make a concerted effort to put an end to their egocentrism and realize that they live in a society. Then, and only then, will the truth be accorded the proper respect.

Quiz 1

1. **On what block of Park Avenue do the McCoys live?**
   A. Midtown
   B. The 60s
   C. The 70s
   D. The 80s

2. **When Sherman dials his home number by mistake, while out walking the dog, whom does he ask for?**
   A. Bonita
   B. Campbell
   C. Detective Martin
   D. Maria

3. **Where is Sherman and Judy's second home?**
   A. Newport
   B. Long Island
   C. Bucks County
   D. Connecticut

4. **What major life event has just happened to ADA Kramer?**
   A. The birth of his daughter
   B. His mother has died
   C. The birth of his son
   D. He just got a new job

5. **What do Sherman and Maria call Maria's illegally sublet apartment?**
   A. The den
   B. The hiding place
   C. The secret
   D. The hideaway

6. **Where did Thomas Killian attend law school?**
   A. Harvard
   B. Columbia
   C. City College of New York
   D. Yale

7. **What is one of the slang terms for an Irish person in this novel?**

A. Pig

B. Bear

C. Deer

D. Harp

8. **What is the Favor Bank?**

A. A new Irish bank opened in the Bronx.

B. A system of exchange in lieu of money within the prison system.

C. The system of favors used between personnel involved in the criminal justice system.

D. A system of hospitality among Park Avenue WASPs.

9. **Talliaferro is the school Campbell attends. How is it pronounced?**

A. Tallyfer

B. Tolliver

C. Toliafiro

D. Tallaf

10. **What is the name of the firm for which Sherman works?**

A. Pierce and Pierce

B. Dunning, Sponget, and Leach

C. The All–People's Action Fund

D. Gospel Episcopal Church of Harlem

11. **Reverend Bacon was ordained by whom?**

A. The pope

B. The Catholic bishop of New York

C. His mother

D. The Episcopal bishop of New York

12. **In what part of New York do Maria and Sherman get lost?**

A. Harlem

B. Westchester County

C. The Bronx

D. Brooklyn

13. **What kind of car does Sherman drive?**
   A. A Jaguar
   B. A Cadillac
   C. A Mercedes
   D. A Mercury station wagon

14. **When the boys approach Sherman and Maria, what does Sherman think they say?**
   A. Why are you here in the Bronx?
   B. Give us all your money!
   C. Do you need help?
   D. What are you doing?

15. **How much money has the Episcopal Diocese given Reverend Bacon for the Little Shepherd Daycare Center?**
   A. $500.000
   B. $350,000
   C. $980,000
   D. A million dollars

16. **How does Lawrence Kramer meet the girl with brown lipstick?**
   A. She's a defendant in a trial he's prosecuting
   B. She's a judge
   C. She's another prosecutor
   D. She's on a jury in a trial he's prosecuting

17. **What is Mrs. Lamb's relationship to Reverend Bacon?**
   A. She's his former wife.
   B. She used to work for him.
   C. Reverend Bacon is Henry's father.
   D. She doesn't know him at all.

18. **What sort of exercise does Judy McCoy do?**
   A. Long–distance running
   B. Bicycling
   C. Sports Training classes
   D. Ballet

19. **What, in Sherman McCoy's profession, is a "print"?**
   A. A request for a new bond issue
   B. A published novel
   C. A completed transaction
   D. A column in the newspaper

20. **From what country is Peter Fallow?**
   A. United States
   B. England
   C. Australia
   D. Canada

21. **What is the bar that Peter Fallow frequents?**
   A. Le Cirque
   B. Balthazar
   C. Leicester's
   D. Tavern on the Green

22. **What is Lawrence Kramer's wife's name?**
   A. Bonita
   B. Shelly
   C. Judy
   D. Rhoda

23. **Why does Kramer wear his running shoes in to work?**
   A. He likes to look like his defendants.
   B. For health and fitness.
   C. He doesn't have any dress shoes.
   D. To be able to run away from dangerous criminals.

24. **The Bavardages throw what kind of a party?**
   A. A dinner party
   B. A cocktail party
   C. A luncheon
   D. A ball

25. **Why is Herbert 92X so named?**

A. He is a foundling and has no other name.
B. That is the number of his criminal trial.
C. That is his number in the police blotter.
D. It is his Muslim name, like Malcolm X.

Quiz 1 Answer Key

1. **(C)** The 70s
2. **(D)** Maria
3. **(B)** Long Island
4. **(C)** The birth of his son
5. **(D)** The hideaway
6. **(D)** Yale
7. **(D)** Harp
8. **(C)** The system of favors used between personnel involved in the criminal justice system.
9. **(B)** Tolliver
10. **(A)** Pierce and Pierce
11. **(C)** His mother
12. **(C)** The Bronx
13. **(C)** A Mercedes
14. **(C)** Do you need help?
15. **(B)** $350,000
16. **(D)** She's on a jury in a trial he's prosecuting
17. **(B)** She used to work for him.
18. **(C)** Sports Training classes
19. **(C)** A completed transaction
20. **(B)** England
21. **(C)** Leicester's
22. **(D)** Rhoda
23. **(D)** To be able to run away from dangerous criminals.
24. **(A)** A dinner party
25. **(D)** It is his Muslim name, like Malcolm X.

Quiz 2

1. **Who runs the Little Shepherd Day Care Center organization?**
   A. Reverend Bacon
   B. Edward Fiske III
   C. The Episcopal Bishop of New York
   D. Mrs. Annie Lamb

2. **What trees are in the backyard of Reverend Bacon's house?**
   A. Maples
   B. Sycamores
   C. Oaks
   D. Elms

3. **How does Sherman obtain the tape he uses in court to get his case dismissed?**
   A. It's completely fabricated.
   B. The landlord illegally recorded his tenants at Maria's lovenest.
   C. He is "wired."
   D. Quigley records it.

4. **Where is Maria when Sherman is arrested?**
   A. Lake Como, Italy
   B. New York
   C. With her husband
   D. Paris

5. **With what other man is Maria having an affair with besides Sherman?**
   A. Reverend Bacon
   B. Thomas Killian
   C. Fillippo Chirazzi
   D. The Mayor of New York

6. **What animal is Campbell writing about when Sherman visits her in her room?**
   A. A horse
   B. A dog
   C. A teddy bear
   D. A koala

7. **Where did Judy and Sherman live before they moved to Park Avenue?**
   A. Harlem
   B. Tribeca
   C. Lower Manhattan
   D. The Village

8. **What amount does Thomas Killian ask for for a retainer?**
   A. $10,000
   B. $50,000
   C. $75,000
   D. $100,000

9. **What does Larry Kramer call the Criminal Courts building in the Bronx?**
   A. The Rock
   B. Alcatraz
   C. The Island
   D. Gibraltar

10. **Where does Sherman first try to record a conversation with Maria?**
   A. In the car
   B. Arthur Ruskin's funeral
   C. The airport
   D. The hideaway

11. **What is Quigley's occupation?**
   A. Bond salesman
   B. Investigator employed by Thomas Killian.
   C. Bodyguard employed by Thomas Killian.
   D. Police detective

12. **What is the name of the shoeshine man in Sherman's office?**
   A. Dan
   B. Taliaferro
   C. Eddie
   D. Felix

13. **Where is the hidden tape recorder in Maria's sublet?**

A. The answering machine

B. The floorboards

C. The light fixture

D. The intercom

14. **Why is it illegal to sublet the apartment Maria uses?**

A. It is a rent–controlled apartment, and as long as the tenant stays the rent cannot be raised.

B. Maria is not a US citizen.

C. It is a rent–stabilized duplex.

D. It is a tax–free building used for a non–profit.

15. **What park does Park Avenue face?**

A. Gramercy Park

B. Ozone Park

C. Central Park

D. Battery Park

16. **What is Sherman's alma mater?**

A. Harvard

B. Princeton

C. Dartmouth

D. Yale

17. **Of what country is the bond issue of the Giscard deal?**

A. The United States

B. The United Kingdom

C. Ivory Coast

D. France

18. **To what occupation does Judy McCoy aspire?**

A. Interior decorator

B. Painter

C. Fashion designer

D. Dancer

19. **Who could be considered Sherman's only real friend in this novel, outside of his family?**
    A. Rawlie Thorpe
    B. Marshall the dachshund
    C. Eddie the doorman
    D. Gene Lopwitz

20. **What insects, hidden in the firewood, bit Gene Lopwitz?**
    A. Beetles
    B. Spiders
    C. Chiggers
    D. Mosquitos

21. **What essential articles of clothing do they take from Sherman in the "holding pen"?**
    A. His coat and tie
    B. His shoes and socks
    C. His belt and his shoelaces
    D. His hat and overcoat

22. **Who is Bonita?**
    A. The McCoy's nanny.
    B. The McCoy's housekeeper.
    C. Maria Ruskin's lady's maid.
    D. The caretaker at the Southampton house.

23. **Why is Dan the garage attendant suspicious of Sherman?**
    A. Dan is African–American.
    B. Sherman is overly friendly with him.
    C. He comes home the night of the accident smelling of alcohol.
    D. He comes home the night of the accident with his jacket ripped.

24. **What is Peter Fallow's addiction?**
    A. Heroin
    B. Cocaine
    C. Alcohol
    D. Gambling

25. **Why is Gerald Steiner's nickname?**

A. The Publisher
B. Gibraltar
C. The Big Boss
D. The Dead Mouse

Quiz 2 Answer Key

1. **(A)** Reverend Bacon
2. **(B)** Sycamores
3. **(B)** The landlord illegally recorded his tenants at Maria's lovenest.
4. **(A)** Lake Como, Italy
5. **(C)** Fillippo Chirazzi
6. **(D)** A koala
7. **(D)** The Village
8. **(C)** $75,000
9. **(D)** Gibraltar
10. **(B)** Arthur Ruskin's funeral
11. **(B)** Investigator employed by Thomas Killian.
12. **(D)** Felix
13. **(D)** The intercom
14. **(A)** It is a rent–controlled apartment, and as long as the tenant stays the rent cannot be raised.
15. **(C)** Central Park
16. **(D)** Yale
17. **(D)** France
18. **(A)** Interior decorator
19. **(A)** Rawlie Thorpe
20. **(C)** Chiggers
21. **(C)** His belt and his shoelaces
22. **(B)** The McCoy's housekeeper.
23. **(D)** He comes home the night of the accident with his jacket ripped.
24. **(C)** Alcohol
25. **(D)** The Dead Mouse

Quiz 3

1. **In what division of the DA's office does Kramer work?**
   A. Racketeering
   B. Homicide
   C. Drug Squad
   D. Vice

2. **Why didn't Sherman's case ever come to trial?**
   A. Thomas Killian prevented it through legal trickery.
   B. The Mayor granted a pardon.
   C. Because there was suspicion about Maria's testimony.
   D. Judge Kovitsky was bribed.

3. **What award does Fallow win for his coverage of the McCoy case?**
   A. Pulitzer
   B. Nobel
   C. Oscar
   D. National Book Award

4. **Where do Judy and Campbell hide while there is rioting in front of their apartment on Fifth Avenue?**
   A. The Southhampton House.
   B. At the Bavardages.
   C. Sherman's parents' house.
   D. With Judy's parents in Wisconsin.

5. **On the beach in Southhampton, what does Campbell ask her father?**
   A. Why the police are after him.
   B. Whether or not Santa exists.
   C. If there is a God.
   D. What he does for a living.

6. **What is the main problem, for Larry, in his relationship with Shelly Thomas?**
   A. She doesn't admire his trial skills enough.
   B. Larry is still married.
   C. They have no where to meet.
   D. She has a boyfriend.

7. **Who is "Pimp"?**
   A. A murderer brought into the Bronx precinct house.
   B. The man who manages Maria's prostitution business.
   C. A nickname for Henry Lamb.
   D. Maria's younger brother.

8. **What happens to Peter Fallow after the collapsed Arthur Ruskin is taken away?**
   A. He immediately calls Arthur's wife.
   B. He is overcome with remorse.
   C. The waiter presents him with the bill.
   D. He is called immediately back to The City Light.

9. **Who is the publisher of The City Light?**
   A. Arthur Ruskin
   B. Sir Gerald Steiner
   C. John Campbell McCoy
   D. Albert Vogel

10. **At the end of the novel, to whom is Peter Fallow married?**
    A. Sir Gerald Steiner's daughter
    B. Judy McCoy
    C. Mona
    D. Maria Ruskin

11. **In the Epilogue, what hand signal does Sherman give to his wife?**
    A. A beckon.
    B. A wave.
    C. The "Black Power" raised fist.
    D. The thumbs–up.

12. **Why doesn't Killian represent McCoy in the reopened criminal trial?**
    A. Killian says there is no chance of winning.
    B. Killian has grow to dislike Sherman.
    C. Sherman no longer has the money to retain him.
    D. Sherman's new counsel is Al Vogel.

13. **Of what race is the Bishop of the Episcopal Diocese of New York?**
   A. Asian–American
   B. Native American
   C. African–American
   D. Caucasian

14. **What henchman of Reverend Bacon's appears at both the riot in the beginning and the end of the novel?**
   A. Roland Auburn
   B. Annie Lamb
   C. Henry Lamb
   D. The tall man with the gold earring

15. **What is John Campbell McCoy's occupation?**
   A. Doctor
   B. Lawyer
   C. Bond salesman
   D. Businessman

16. **What is Bobby Shaflett's occupation?**
   A. Lawyer
   B. Bond salesman
   C. Criminal
   D. Opera singer

17. **Whom does Sherman call "Social X Rays"?**
   A. The hired help.
   B. The women in the Bronx.
   C. Maria's friends from the South.
   D. Extremely thin society ladies.

18. **Who coins the phrase "Weiss Justice is White Justice"?**
   A. Al Vogel
   B. Reverend Bacon
   C. The Mayor
   D. Peter Fallow

19. **What tipped off the detectives that Sherman was involved?**
   A. The eyewitnesses who saw the crash.
   B. The evidence on the car.
   C. Maria Ruskin's evidence.
   D. His nervous manner when they interviewed him.

20. **What kind of defendants does Killian's firm often represent?**
   A. Wall Street insider traders
   B. Indigents
   C. Racketeers
   D. Drug dealers

21. **What does Sherman often overhear Killian discussing with his clients?**
   A. Their feelings.
   B. Their ability to pay him.
   C. The states of their criminal defenses.
   D. Their family lives.

22. **On their second meeting, where does Al Vogel take Peter Fallow?**
   A. A Chinese restaurant.
   B. Reverend Bacon's house.
   C. The Ritz–Carlton.
   D. The Bronx County building.

23. **For the arrival of whom are the staff of La Boue D'Argent preparing when Fallow and Arthur Ruskin arrive?**
   A. Reverend Bacon
   B. The Mayor of New York
   C. Madame Tacaya
   D. Sherman McCoy

24. **To what does Judy liken the profits from Sherman's bond sales?**
   A. Golden apples
   B. Golden crumbs
   C. Golden tickets
   D. Ill–gotten gains

25. **From what country is Sherman's fellow bond salesman, Arguello?**

A. Mexico
B. Columbia
C. Argentina
D. Spain

Quiz 3 Answer Key

1. **(B)** Homicide
2. **(C)** Because there was suspicion about Maria's testimony.
3. **(A)** Pulitzer
4. **(C)** Sherman's parents' house.
5. **(D)** What he does for a living.
6. **(C)** They have no where to meet.
7. **(A)** A murderer brought into the Bronx precinct house.
8. **(C)** The waiter presents him with the bill.
9. **(B)** Sir Gerald Steiner
10. **(A)** Sir Gerald Steiner's daughter
11. **(C)** The "Black Power" raised fist.
12. **(C)** Sherman no longer has the money to retain him.
13. **(C)** African–American
14. **(D)** The tall man with the gold earring
15. **(B)** Lawyer
16. **(D)** Opera singer
17. **(D)** Extremely thin society ladies.
18. **(B)** Reverend Bacon
19. **(D)** His nervous manner when they interviewed him.
20. **(D)** Drug dealers
21. **(B)** Their ability to pay him.
22. **(A)** A Chinese restaurant.
23. **(C)** Madame Tacaya
24. **(B)** Golden crumbs
25. **(C)** Argentina

Quiz 4

1. **How, in bond salesman's parlance, is a deal involving $1 million in a bond sale called?**
    A. 1.0 bonds
    B. One million bonds
    C. One M of bonds
    D. One million of bonds

2. **What does Sherman believe Freddy Button to be?**
    A. In league with Reverend Bacon
    B. Gay
    C. Lying
    D. Having an affair with Maria Ruskin

3. **What is John Campbell McCoy's reaction when he learns that Sherman has gone to Freddy Button for help?**
    A. Fear
    B. Resentment
    C. Anger
    D. Shock

4. **Who is the "Last of the Great Smokers"?**
    A. Freddy Button
    B. Lawrence Kramer
    C. John Campbell McCoy
    D. The Mayor of New York

5. **In what area of the Bronx does Shelly Thomas live?**
    A. Gibraltar
    B. Ozone Park
    C. Riverdale
    D. South Bronx

6. **What do Peter Fallow and his friends call the Americans who buy them drinks?**
    A. Suckers
    B. Lads
    C. Fish
    D. Dupes

7. **How does Sherman eventually manage to extricate himself from the original court case?**
   A. He tapes Maria
   B. He listens to his wife
   C. He bribes the judge
   D. He lies on the stand

8. **What is Bernie Fitzgibbon's occupation?**
   A. Chief of the Homicide Bureau
   B. Beat cop
   C. Criminal Courts judge
   D. Homocide detective

9. **What is Abe Weiss running for?**
   A. Reelection to DA of the Bronx
   B. For Governor of New York
   C. President of the Yale Club
   D. For Mayor of New York

10. **Why did Thomas Killian give up jogging?**
   A. It hurt his back.
   B. He had too much work on McCoy's case.
   C. He was mugged.
   D. His wife disliked it.

11. **Besides church founder, what was Reverend Bacon's mother's occupation?**
   A. Gospel singer
   B. She worked for the marriage bureau
   C. She worked for the Mayor
   D. Policewoman

12. **What enraged Sherman the most when the detectives visited his home?**
   A. They leered at his wife.
   B. Goldberg sat on his desk.
   C. They insulted his housekeeper.
   D. Martin mistook his name for an Irish name.

13. **Gene Lopwitz, in addition to running Pierce &Pierce, is a:**
    A. Homophobe
    B. Agoraphobe
    C. Anglophile
    D. Bibliophile

14. **What does Sherman do with Campbell each weekday morning?**
    A. Drives her to school.
    B. Tells her a story.
    C. Walks her to the bus stop.
    D. Feeds her breakfast.

15. **When things get difficult for Sherman, to what state does he wish to retreat?**
    A. Pennsylvania
    B. Florida
    C. Tennessee
    D. Connecticut

16. **What is fundamentally wrong in Thomas Killian's office?**
    A. There are no windows.
    B. No one speaks English.
    C. The lights are far too bright.
    D. The receptionist is rude.

17. **By what method does Maria try to incite envy in other women in the airport?**
    A. The looks of her lover
    B. Her knowledge of Christopher Marlowe.
    C. Her art expertise.
    D. Her expensive and glamorous clothing.

18. **When does Sherman finally tell Judy about the accident?**
    A. A couple of days later.
    B. The night before he will be arrested.
    C. When she meets Maria at the Bavardages.
    D. The day it happened.

19. **In jail, Sherman and the other prisoners have what for lunch?**
   A. Fruit and nuts
   B. Hotdogs and coke
   C. Koolaid and sandwiches
   D. Cheese pizza

20. **Whom does Sherman call "Lemon Tarts"?**
   A. Reverend Bacon's followers
   B. Shelly Thomas and Annie Lamb
   C. Al Vogel's girlfriends
   D. The young, usually blonde women dated by old rich men.

21. **On what street does Roland Auburn say the accident took place?**
   A. 110th Street
   B. Park Avenue
   C. Wall Street
   D. Bruckner Boulevard

22. **What animal does Sherman liken his father to?**
   A. A bear
   B. A lion
   C. A wolf
   D. An owl

23. **What is Sherman's mother's name?**
   A. Celeste
   B. Penelope
   C. Judy
   D. Annie

24. **Why does Larry Kramer take the subway to work?**
   A. There is no other way to get to the Bronx County Building.
   B. He enjoys danger.
   C. He can't afford a car.
   D. He likes to be near his defendants.

25. **Where does Peter Fallow keep his liquor at the office?**

A. In the pocket of his raincoat.

B. Locked in a desk drawer.

C. In his in–box.

D. Under Gerald Steiner's desk.

Quiz 4 Answer Key

1. **(B)** One million bonds
2. **(B)** Gay
3. **(D)** Shock
4. **(A)** Freddy Button
5. **(C)** Riverdale
6. **(C)** Fish
7. **(A)** He tapes Maria
8. **(A)** Chief of the Homicide Bureau
9. **(A)** Reelection to DA of the Bronx
10. **(A)** It hurt his back.
11. **(A)** Gospel singer
12. **(B)** Goldberg sat on his desk.
13. **(C)** Anglophile
14. **(C)** Walks her to the bus stop.
15. **(C)** Tennessee
16. **(C)** The lights are far too bright.
17. **(D)** Her expensive and glamorous clothing.
18. **(B)** The night before he will be arrested.
19. **(C)** Koolaid and sandwiches
20. **(D)** The young, usually blonde women dated by old rich men.
21. **(D)** Bruckner Boulevard
22. **(B)** A lion
23. **(A)** Celeste
24. **(C)** He can't afford a car.
25. **(A)** In the pocket of his raincoat.

Printed in Great Britain
by Amazon

57757793R00077